I0796722

# The Rise and Fall of Rotha Lintorn-Orman

My thanks go to my wife Isabel for her tireless patience, and to my friend and fellow researcher Philip Crawford.

# The Rise and Fall of Rotha Lintorn-Orman

## From Serving in WWI to Founding Britain's First Fascist Party

**Anthony J. Randall**

AN IMPRINT OF PEN & SWORD BOOKS LTD.
YORKSHIRE – PHILADELPHIA

First published in Great Britain in 2025 by
Pen & Sword History
An imprint of
Pen & Sword Books Ltd
Yorkshire - Philadelphia



ISBN 978 1 03613 495 2



A CIP catalogue record for this book is available from the British Library.



Typeset in INDIA by IMPEC eSolutions
Printed and bound in England by CPI (UK) Ltd.

The Publisher's authorised representative in the EU for product safety is Authorised Rep Compliance Ltd., Ground Floor, 71 Lower Baggot Street, Dublin D02 P593, Ireland.
www.arccompliance.com

For a complete list of Pen & Sword titles please contact:

PEN & SWORD BOOKS LIMITED
47 Church Street, Barnsley, South Yorkshire, S70 2AS, England
E-mail: enquiries@pen-and-sword.co.uk
Website: www.pen-and-sword.co.uk

or

PEN AND SWORD BOOKS
1950 Lawrence Rd, Havertown, PA 19083, USA
E-mail: uspen-and-sword@casematepublishers.com
Website: www.penandswordbooks.com

# Contents

*Chapter 1*

# Cornwall Gardens

The select garden squares in London stand as a monument to the late Victorian age. Elegant green areas in the very centre of the metropolis, providing shade during the heat of summer and space for young families to play. Not of course working class families, but upper-middle class children with their nannies, perhaps with their mother sitting on an adjacent bench reading a novel. Couples walking across the green sward, he in formal daytime attire, she carrying her parasol. A scene that might be echoed in the European enclaves of Bombay or Delhi, where the Saabs and Memsaabs would be interspersed with the military types of the British Raj.

This was the world in which our story begins, a world of privilege and comfort, a world that is populated by men and women who are certain of who and what they are. Queen Victoria was on the throne, the British Empire held sway over the whole world and the British Navy was a 'force to be reckoned with'. British democracy was the envy of the world and the established British social order of upper, middle and working classes worked to the satisfaction of all; and there were few in Kensington who would disagree with that.

The working class showed deference to the middle class, and the middle class to the upper. This was a microcosm of the British Empire; the British in charge, the educated locals acting as administrators, the uneducated locals providing the labour. Between the two extremes were Canada, Australia, New Zealand and South Africa, holding Dominion status but still owing allegiance to the British crown. However, the established structure was under strain, newer ideas were being voiced, and fresh minds were being brought to bear on the subject. A European war was feared, even being anticipated in some quarters, with a change to the established social order being in prospect.

In early February 1895 the scene in London was very different from that which might have been experienced on the Indian sub-continent. On the 7th of that month the temperature fell to -21.7 °C, with Londoners taking to their skates on the Serpentine, and ice flows on the Thames hindering shipping. Deaths from hypothermia among the poor were rising and the incidence of pneumonia and other respiratory diseases was increasing at an alarming rate. In the intense cold there was little snow, forcing the frost deep into the ground with the consequential fracturing of water pipes which was inconvenient, and of the public gas supply which was deadly.

Cornwall Gardens in Kensington, lying only one mile south of the Serpentine lake in Hyde Park, showed a very different face than it had done during the previous summer. No nannies sat shivering with their charges, no children played on the frosted grass, and no mothers sat reading their afternoon away, turning each page with a mittened hand. Even the perimeter footpath, which seemed to be the hallmark of all the London public gardens, was devoid of footprints or perambulator tracks in the frost; small children were kept safely indoors.

The elegant houses that surrounded Cornwall Gardens stood stark against the winter sky. Windows were shuttered and curtained against the cold; roof tiles dripped with melted snow and icicles as a testament to the poor insulation of the servants' rooms in the attic space, only to form ice stalactites as they froze again below the cast iron guttering. The steps running from the pavement down to the underground kitchen were treacherous to pedestrians, servants and tradesmen alike, and to be traversed only with the greatest caution.

Rotha Beryl Lintorn Orman chose 7 February 1895 to announce her arrival into what could be a very cold and hostile world, but her first cries were confined to the warm and cosy interior of 36 Cornwall Gardens, helped by a doctor and a midwife and two housemaids.[1] Her father, Charles Edward Orman, was informed of her birth only when all was clean and orderly. Her mother, Blanch Orman, was sitting up in bed with her hair tidied and her bed jacket un-crumpled, when she and her daughter were presented to Captain Charles Edward Orman of the 1st Essex Regiment.

The house in which Rotha was born stood on the north side of Cornwall Gardens, on the opposite side of the road to the beautiful hexagonal Victorian Penfold bright red post box that still graces the Square. The Ormans lived at No 36 Cornwall Gardens, built about twenty years before Rotha's birth, an elegant town residence. The main entrance was approached by a short flight of wide steps, leading through a porch which was supported by four elegant stone pillars. However, this was not Charles Ormans' house but the London residence of Blanch's parents, John Simmons and his wife, also named Blanch.

Charles Orman and Blanch Simmons had been married on 5 September 1893 at St Stephen's Church in Kensington, after the banns had been read for the stipulated three Sundays, as required by law.[2] Charles Orman, thirty-three years old, and born at Roorkee in India to Major and Mrs Orman of the Bengal Staff Corps, was living alone in the South Kensington Hotel, a short distance away. He had been commissioned in 1878 from the Royal Military College Sandhurst, and then joined the Essex Regiment (44th Foot), spending just one short tour of duty in the East Indies before returning to home shores.

Charles' father, also Charles Edward, was an army major and his mother, Isabella Jane Hawthorne, was born in Cawnpore Bengal, the child of another military family. Charles was one of eleven children, only seven of which lived to adulthood; one child was born in Great Yarmouth, while on leave, but all the others were born in various parts of India. Charles senior 'was the magistrate at Roorkee and died there in 1872 having caught sunstroke after a long hot day on his elephant, which got stuck in sand'.[3]

Following his death Isabella returned to Britain with her children, some quite young. Isabella was quite well connected and financially sound, so the younger children found themselves either at private schools or living with family members and being taught by governesses. The Orman family was larger than that of the Simmons and definitely not a nuclear family, as we understand that term today. Rotha's father appears to have had little to with his own mother once back in England, and there is little indication of Rotha having any real connection with her father's extended family.

Charles' mother, Isabella, and his two sisters, Mabel and Minerva, known in the family as Minnie, were living at 62 St. Quintin Avenue, also in Kensington, but a little further north than the Simmons' town residence.[4] When Isabella had been widowed twenty years previously, and then had returned to Britain, she had brought Charles' younger brother, John Julius Hawthorne Orman, with her; he carried his mother's maiden surname as his third given name.

Quintin Avenue was not as prestigious an address as Cornwall Gardens, yet could be regarded as very respectable and home to affluent upper-middle class families. Isabella's immediate neighbours included a diamond broker and a commission merchant on one side and various ladies with private means on the other. In such a neighbourhood, all had the benefit of live-in servants to a greater or lesser degree. However, the different strata of society were even more pronounced than today and 'service' represented a significant portion of the gross national product.

Being in Service was a very usual practice for young women and it is estimated that a third of girls aged between fifteen and twenty years old were employed in domestic service. Indeed in 1900 domestic service provided a standard of living beyond what might be expected if living at home and working in any other industry. By the standards of the day, domestic service meant somewhere warm and dry to live, adequate food and a life outside the dreaded workhouse.

Rotha Beryl Lintorn Orman was Charles and Blanch's first, and their only, child. The dominant family in the young girl's life was to be that of her mother, rather than that of her father, and it would be her maternal grandfather who offered Rotha and her parents financial security following his death in 1903. Field-Marshal John Lintorn Arabin Simmons was a force to be reckoned with and he was able to offer Captain Orman's wife and daughter much more than they could have expected from a captain in the Essex Regiment.

It's not clear how the couple met, but the most likely explanation is that both Charles Orman and John Lintorn Arabin Simmons were at the Royal Military College at the same time; the former as a student, the latter as an instructor. It would be unfair to cast any doubts upon the motives of the younger of the two by observing the impact that such a marriage could have upon the career of a young officer; it could be to his real advantage, but there is no real evidence to suggest that Charles Orman was not just a young man in love. When the time came of course Charles was more than happy to reap the financial rewards of 'good' marriage.

In 1893, at the time of her marriage, Blanch Simmons had given her address as 36 Cornwall Gardens, where she and her parents lived in a household served by five domestic staff, including a single ladies' maid who was shared by Blanch and her mother. After the marriage, rather than setting up in a home of their own, Charles Orman joined the Simmons family to live at 36 Cornwall Gardens, which was given as Charles' regular home address when he registered the birth, just over a year later.

John Lintorn Arabin Simmons, the baby's grandfather, was born 12 February 1821 at Lower Langford in Somerset and baptised 11 April at the parish church in the nearby village of Churchill,[5] a parish that dates from medieval times. During the eighteenth and nineteenth century much of the surrounding countryside was the subject of the Inclosure Acts of the period. Since then the locality had been given over almost entirely to grazing. The family home of Over Langford Manor, prior to the Simmons ownership, had served as one of the courthouses presided over by the infamous Judge Jeffreys, the 'hanging judge', following the Monmouth Rebellion of 1685. Previously to that, during the English Civil War, Over Langford Manor had raised soldiers for Cromwell's Model Army.

Over Langford Manor, constructed of the local limestone, lies on the Bath Road not far from Churchill village. The land backs onto the Mendip Hills, a soft undulating landscape given over mainly to grazing, with fields delineated by ancient dry stone walls. It enjoys what the Irish would term a 'soft' climate; plentiful rain ensures luxurious grazing, but beneath the pastureland, an underlying rock allows the water to spill down into the rivers and streams that lie in the valleys below.

Coming from a military background, John Simmons had been commissioned in 1845 and then served in Canada; he returned to Britain where he took up a post at the Royal Military Academy in Woolwich and was then awarded a number of prestigious appointments under the Board of Trade, with special responsibility for railways. He served in the Turkish/Russian war of 1854, including the defence of Silistra, and in the Siege of Sevastopol in 1855; he was later appointed as the British Consul in Warsaw.

On his return to Britain, he was promoted to major-general and then given a range of promotions within the Royal Military College, finally reaching the rank of lieutenant-general and then full general. In 1884 he served as Governor of Malta and, on his retirement, ended his career with the rank of field-marshal. He then moved to Hawley House in Hampshire, an elegant eighteenth century country mansion, which he held on lease, standing in sixty acres of parkland. Simmons was a wealthy man; he had a mansion in Hampshire, a rural retreat in Somerset and a town residence in Kensington.

Hawley House and the parkland around it date from the late eighteenth century, complete with a walled garden, greenhouses, a stable block, a summerhouse and three lodges; there was also an area of woodland within the seventeen acre estate. The village of Hawley adjoins the town of Blackwater and lies very close to Farnborough.

Physically, Sir Lintorn Simmons, who had been awarded a knighthood in 1869, was an imposing figure. It was at this time that he decided to drop the name John and was thereafter known as Lintorn Arabin Simmons, a name more in keeping with his elevated status. His most dominant feature was his large and impressive moustache which was expertly groomed, and draws the eye of all who look upon his likeness. This is demonstrated by a reproduction of his portrait hanging on the wall of Saint Mary's Church in Langford, a church and village to whom he was a significant benefactor.

His portrait by Giuseppe Cali pictures him in full dress uniform sporting his famous moustache and side whiskers, a characteristic that was also the dominant feature in the 1877 cartoon of him by Leslie Ward, published in the *Vanity Fair* magazine. Giuseppe Cali also painted Simmons' second wife Blanch, in a more relaxed pose with muted colours, presenting a softer image of this military family. By all accounts, the field-marshal's wife was a woman with a forceful character, yet with a sympathetic nature, traits that were displayed by her daughter Blanch.

Rotha's mother, Blanch Simmons, became a personal friend of the Empress Eugenie, the wife of Napoleon III, and by extension this friendship also included Mademoiselle Blanch, as the Empress referred to Lady Simmons' daughter. The Empress Eugenie was already an old lady of seventy by the time that Rotha was born, a widow for more than twenty years and had chosen Farnborough as her final home where, coincidently, she had financed a military hospital during the war.

In the years before her marriage, Blanch Simmons, later Orman, had accompanied her father on numerous official overseas visits, and her diaries of that time have since been published. The diaries record two trips taken by Blanch and her parents in 1879 and 1880. The first, a family holiday to Belgium and the Netherlands; the second, an official trip to Germany in order to attend a conference in Berlin.

Blanch Simmons, Rotha's mother, was the only child from John Lintorn Simmons' second marriage. His first marriage, to Ellen Lintorn Simmons, had also produced a daughter named Eleanor who was living at Walton in Somerset, close to the family home. John and Ellen were cousins, each bearing the name Lintorn, and it may be that familial connection that was one of the factors that caused Eleanor to be extremely short-sighted, to the extent that it is identified on her census return of 1891.[6] Here she lived alone with two domestic servants who attended her and any visiting guests.

Rotha had been born into a world of privilege, but a world that was still very limited in what it could provide for a newborn child. This was a world where, on a cold day in February, a person was heated by a fire in the room in which they were seated, whatever warmth they felt came from the direction of the fireplace, the flames heated their face, not their back. The concept of central heating, except for the very grand houses, was still limited and still some way into the future, even for wealthy households. The nursery was warm, of course, as were the bedrooms and reception rooms, but the corridors and passages, the scullery and the boot room, and certainly the servants' living quarters, were all heated by the warmth which escaped the family.

Elsewhere in Britain, and in the wider world, events were taking place that would have repercussions for the girl just born. Robert Baden-Powell had recently published his book, *Reconnaissance and Scouting*,[7] in which he wrote that knowledge of the enemy and the geography of the countryside held the key to success in war. The book included chapters on practical map drawing, calculating angles and distances, horse riding and many other topics. Although aimed at a readership of military men, there was some interest in the civilian world, particularly from young men and even boys with an eye for adventure and a military career. Baden-Powell would prove to have a significant influence on the life that Rotha would later lead.

Although his death would come when Rotha was just five years old, the Irish poet and playwright Oscar Wilde, would have an indirect yet significant influence on the life she would lead. He was in prison during the first three years of Rotha's life, and had no direct contact with ether the Simmons or Orman families, but his unusual lifestyle had, to some extent, opened the door to the possibility of accepting another way of living. Homosexuality between men was still seen as an aberration, but between women was beginning to be viewed as a foolishness and the word 'inverted' became more generally used.

The Marquis of Queensberry, father of Lord Alfred Douglas who had been Wilde's lover, had begun his campaign against Oscar Wilde in 1875 by leaving his calling card at the Albemarle Club, inciting Wilde to sue him for libel. In the courts the Marquis of Queensberry was acquitted and Oscar Wilde subsequently charged with committing acts of gross indecency. Found guilty, Wilde spent time in Holloway, Pentonville and Reading prisons. Wilde had been financially ruined by Queensbury's claim for expenses, and died in penury as an exile in Paris.

For a young girl at the close of the Victorian era there was little to offer outside the home that was not in some way an extension of their existing domestic and religious life. There were, of course, organisations such as the Girls Friendly Society which was formed in 1874 by a group of five ladies meeting in the drawing room of the Archbishop's Palace at Lambeth to 'consider whether anything could be done to protect and befriend young girls, especially girls from country districts, going out to employment in large towns.' The very ethos of the organisation was to reinforce the moral and religious qualities that these ladies of the Church considered desirable in young women.

There were a number of other clubs and societies that were directed towards women, some to girls, but most followed the path laid down by the Girls Friendly Society and the domestic and moral attitudes that were prescribed by their elders. These were following the goals of an older generation, goals of which the older generation approved. There was enjoyment, satisfaction, approval, even piety, but what there was very little of was 'fun'. Little to differentiate the joys of youth from the self-satisfaction of the Victorian lady.

With the end of the Victorians and the anticipation of what the Edwardians would bring, girls and young women would begin to view the world quite differently from how their mothers had done. Horizons would broaden, women's suffrage was not an impossible dream, nursing was taking on a mantle of respectability, young women were working in offices as well as in factories or in the fields, and a different relationship was becoming established between young men and young women.

There was a growing awareness of an issue which was yet to surface in the drawing rooms of late Victorian society. Close to home the Kensington Society had been formed in 1865 as a discussion group and had subsequently presented, via John Stuart Mill, a petition to Parliament calling for women's suffrage. The issue was not resolved in 1865, but women's suffrage was being brought to the fore at the time of Rotha's birth, and would become more significant in the run up to the First World War.

> It surely will not be denied that women have, and ought to have, opinions of their own on subjects of public interest, and on the events which arise as the world wends on its way. But if it be granted that women may,

> without offence, hold political opinions, on what ground can the right be withheld of giving the same expression or effect to their opinions as that enjoyed by their male neighbours?[8]

For the individual, a gradual awareness, even acceptance, of homosexual activity in both men and women was also developing. There was still great opposition to its very existence, let alone its practices, although lesbianism was seen as misguided rather than the abomination that was male homosexuality. Wilde's affair with Lord Alfred Douglas resulted in his prosecution and being sentenced to two years hard labour while women, dressed in men's clothing and sporting fake moustaches, were seen as being emancipated and their behaviour being an expression of 'free untrammelled womanhood' as described by Susan B. Anthony, a women's rights activist in America. There were pairs of women engaged in sexual relationships, but they did not attract the attention that their male counterparts would have received had they have been as explicit.

Hidden in plain sight, there were a significant number of 'butch lesbians' being accepted into mainstream society. Lady Una Vincenzo, the sculptor, only eight years older than Rotha, was to lead a most unconventional life. She dressed and acted as a man and sustained a long term sexual relationship with Marguerite Radclyffe Hall, the author. Much earlier in the century Anne Lister, known as 'Gentleman Jack', became very much the archetypal 'butch lesbian'. This, again, would prove to have a significant influence on the life that Rotha would later embrace.

Blanch Orman played very little part in the practical day-to-day care of Rotha, relying heavily upon the nursemaid. Normal practice at that time was to confine the mother to bed rest for nine to fourteen days after the birth, during which time she would have been more involved with the child's daily routine than she would be for the next few years. Of course there was mother and baby time, but Rotha was primarily the nursemaid's responsibility and would only be presented to her mother, and father, washed and fed and content. Wakeful nights would not be an issue for Blanch and Charles unless Rotha was clearly unwell, when they felt it was their duty to attend.

The unusually cold weather did not break until mid-April and it was only then that the nursemaid could venture out with Rotha, to take a turn around Cornwall Gardens, or one of the other similar garden settlements in the locality. On such walks the infant could gradually become socialised with others in the care of their own nursemaids or nannies. As the summer drew on, Blanch would occasionally sit with them and observe, but Rotha's upbringing really remained the responsibility of their paid employee.

It is worth remembering that these were very different times than today, and that behaviour between parent and child should be judged according to the standards of the time. It was not unusual for a child's early years to be in the charge of a full time nurse or nanny, but something can be learnt of Rotha's earliest years from the background of her mother's own upbringing. Rotha was the product of a late marriage, as was Blanch, her mother, and was the only child of that marriage.

Blanch was brought up isolated from other children, educated at home, and from a military family. As a young woman she was the companion of one parent, in her case her father, and learnt her manner of behaviour directly from him. Now, as a mother herself, her own daughter was to be raised in a very similar environment, in a household of adults who themselves had little experience of a close family life.

## *Chapter 2*

# Hawley House

The weather in London, the cold spell continuing well into spring of 1895, improved significantly to actually produce one of the driest summers on record, followed by a few years of quite unexceptional weather to accompany Rotha's first few years in the world. Life in Cornwall Gardens fell back into its normal comfortable regime of respectability and contentment with the 'status quo'. This was a household which existed as a consequence of John Simmons' standing in society, rather than that of Charles Orman.

Her regular companions at this time were from the upper echelons of society, from within the royal family and its aristocratic circles. Sir Lintorn Simmons moved in such company as this, as did his daughter Blanch, and this spilled over to include Blanch's daughter Rotha, who now carried the name of Orman rather than Simmons. There were occasional family meetings with the younger members of the royal family, including Albert Frederick Arthur George, later to become George VI.

The first major trauma of Rotha's childhood occurred with the death of her maternal grandmother, born Blanch Weston the daughter of a barrister, who had married the widowed John Lintorn Arabin Simmons at All Saints Church, Knightsbridge in 1856.[1] Blanch, seventy-four years old, died in 1898 at her home in Cornwall Gardens, but the family travelled to Over

Langford Manor in Somerset for her funeral and burial at St John the Baptist Church in nearby Churchill.[2] Rotha was three years old, and would have known little of this rather distant old lady, except in her being the matriarch of the Simmons household. The details of the funeral, reported in the *Weston-Super-Mare Gazette*, makes no mention of those who attended, but it is reasonable to assume that a child of Rotha's age would have been left in London, in the care of her nanny.

> During the tenure of Field Marshal Simmons, as Governor of these Islands, the deceased Lady endeared herself to all who knew her, irrespective of rank or station, of creed or nationality, by her unceasing kindness and abundant charity, which is still green in the memory of her legion of friends and grateful dependents.[3]

It is quite possible though, that the traditional practices of the Victorian era were still in play within the Simmons family. The general procedure in those times was that the body of the deceased would be laid out in the family home in order to receive visitors prior to the actual funeral. It would be difficult to hide this fact from the children of the house, indeed they would be expected to behave and dress in keeping with the occasion. Without specific evidence to the contrary it might be assumed that such a situation existed in the Simmons household. However, unless Sir Lintorn insisted, reading ahead to how Charles and Blanch raised their daughter, it is quite reasonable to have expected them to spare Rotha from the trauma of the internment itself.

Churchill and Langford were both served by St John the Baptist church, a significant portion of the congregation being drawn from Langford; for Churchill residents the walk to St John's was a tidy step, for those in Langford, it was something of a trek. Two years after his wife's funeral, Sir Lintorn funded the building of a second church in Langford, dedicated to St Mary, in order that the local population should have access to a more convenient church than St John's each Sunday. The new St Mary's church carries reminders of and dedications to the Simmons family, including stained glass windows depicting members of the family.

It is interesting to consider the design of the two churches. On the one hand, St John the Baptist in Churchill, built in local stone and a little distant from the village, proudly announces its twelfth century origins and its fourteenth century tower; a church to be revered, and a backdrop against which is displayed the major events of the parish. On the other hand St Mary's in Langford is at the centre of the village, built of local brick and has only a *campanile*, with a single bell to call the congregation to prayer.

St John the Baptist church dates from as early as the twelfth century but was thoroughly restored in 1879, again with contributions from the Simmons family. The church stands within its own graveyard, through which runs a winding path leading from the lychgate to the church. To the right of the graveyard, near the perimeter wall lies the Simmons family plot in which Blanch Simmons was buried and her name added to the main family gravestone. The substantial plot, surrounded by a low wrought-iron railing, lies unattended in this rural landscape like so many of the 'old' family graves.

The funeral over, Charles and Blanch Orman continued with their active social life, much of it centred upon the Essex Regiment where they together are mentioned in a number of entertainments where they both, or Blanch alone sometimes, sang at various events for good causes. They must have both been fairly accomplished as, when Blanch and Charles begin to spend less and less time together, Charles continued to perform alone. Blanch was also a frequent contributor to discussions held through the pages of upper class journals.

Charles Orman's name appears as a contributor to the Widows and Orphans Fund in 1899, and published in the *Daily Telegraph*:

> Sir - I have much pleasure in forwarding you cheques to the value of £40 (800 shillings), the proceeds of an entertainment I gave in aid of the Widows and Orphans of officers, non-commissioned, and men who may fall in the Transvaal War. The amount collected exceeded greatly what I expected, and displays the patriotism of the villagers and the people of this neighbourhood. Yours faithfully, Charles E Orman, Hawley House, Blackwater, Hants.[4]

Charles Orman was also a gentleman cricketer, as against being classed as a professional, and had played two games for the county team of Essex in 1896, without experiencing any spectacular achievements. He was clearly a good club player rather than county material; despite being awarded his place as a batsman, his record only shows him as making a total of sixteen runs from his two county games. Nevertheless, his army rank and his wealth allowed him to indulge his sporting interests by playing for a wide range of socially coalesced teams. Cricket must have featured highly in the family as Charles' brother, John Julius, features in the Bedfordshire records, with similar success.

In January 1901, Britain passed from the Victorian into the Edwardian age. The queen's funeral was held on 2 February 1901, just four days before Rotha's sixth birthday, and the country was preparing for great changes as it entered the twentieth century. The funeral parade brought London to a standstill and many of the great families, if they were not integral to the parade or service, were able to rent private rooms along the route from which to observe the spectacle.

Victoria, as had been her custom, spent Christmas at Osborne House on the Isle of Wight. She died there on 22 January 1901. She was carried by ship to Gosport and then by train to Windsor, via Victoria and Paddington stations, and from there to St Georges Chapel by gun carriage. The Queen was eventually interred alongside her husband Albert at Frogmore after two days lying in state.

The monarchy in Britain had been rather a dampening influence since the death of Victoria's husband, Prince Albert, in 1861. She had spent the majority of those forty years secluded from the public gaze, the country prospering in her absence, that there was some who questioned the very need for a monarchy; the Ormans were not among them. There was some speculation on the relationship between Victoria and her servant John Brown, there was even talk of a clandestine marriage, but that ended with Brown's death in 1883.

During the latter part of the century the feelings of the country towards the monarchy had improved a little with Victoria making herself more accessible. Following incidents in Calcutta, public opinion had been assuaged with the Government's direct control in India being increased, while the East India Company's influence became further constrained. While the discontent in India was being contained, although some voices were raised in the calls for independence, Britain's sphere of influence was having to be defended by raw naval power. Although worldwide pressures were putting a strain on British resources, the real danger lay closer to home; one that would call upon all the resources of the country to combat. Political manoeuvres within Europe were beginning to be of concern to the 'establishment'.

A mutual defence pact between Britain, France, and Russia, and a similar treaty between Germany, Austria-Hungary, and Italy were put in place; a hard line that would separate the two power blocs of the coming world war. As the political lines were drawn in Europe, so animosity grew between the populations that stood either side of those lines. The Paris newspaper *Le Figaro* reported that there were extraordinary outbursts of Anglophobia in Germany and that a general hostility towards Britain was increasing daily. Trade between Germany and many countries in the world was suffering, and Russia was threatening to stop the flow of seasonal agricultural labour to help with the German harvest.

While war between Britain and Germany was not yet clearly on the horizon, there was a growing awareness of tension developing between the two blocs. In Britain there was a fear of German militarism, which was dramatically expressed by Erskine Childers in his book *The Riddle of the Sands* involving a German plot to invade the east coast of Britain,[5] a plot that was foiled. Although the story is entirely fictitious, it fed on a growing distrust of Germany's intentions towards Britain and its Empire, both in their deceit and their recruitment of British nationals for nefarious purposes.

More significant in considering Rotha's future role was the growing belief that a German-Jewish conspiracy had forced Britain into the Second Boer War, a belief that had its origins in the fact that Paul Kruger re-equipped the Transvaal army with German supplied Mauser and Martini–Henry rifles. With these weapons, Germany also supplied fifty million rounds of ammunition. As well as light weapons, Germany also supplied Krupp heavy artillery and shells.

Feelings in Britain were further intensified by the sending of the 'Kruger Telegram' by Kaiser Wilhelm II, congratulating the South African Republic on repelling a British raid. The Kaiser was so angry about the raid, putting German subjects at risk, that he tried to persuade Tsar Nicholas II of Russia to join an anti-British alliance. Although the telegram was applauded in Germany, it caused considerable consternation in Britain, simply feeding anti-German sentiment.

The situation in Britain, Russia and Germany was particularly strange because King George V, Tsar Nicholas II and Kaiser Wilhelm II were all cousins, having common antecedents in the persons of Prince Albert and Queen Victoria, now nearing the end of her life. The Romanovs and the British royal family were particularly close but there was a degree of public scepticism in that Alexandra, the Tsar's wife, was a German at a time when anti-German sympathies were beginning to run high.

Relations between Britain and the Kaiser were strained by a feeling in Britain that Germany was looking towards the British Empire with envy enough to threaten its very existence, as intimated in an address by the Kaiser in 1901.

> In spite of the fact that we have no such fleet as we should have, we have conquered for ourselves a place in the sun. It will now be my task to see to it that this place in the sun shall remain our undisputed possession . . . when the German has once learned to direct his glance upon what is distant and great . . . whoever wishes to have this larger and freer outlook can find no better place than one of the Hanseatic cities . . . we are now making efforts to do what, in the old time, the Hanseatic cities could not accomplish because they lacked the vivifying and protecting power of the empire. . . I therefore rejoice over every citizen, whether from Hamburg, Bremen, or Lübeck, who goes forth . . . and seeks new points where we can drive in the nail on which to hang our armour.[6]

For Rotha's family the death of her grandmother in 1898 had been the catalyst for change. The large house in Cornwall Gardens was vacated and then later occupied by a barrister named William Carr, his wife and their five children, plus staff.

Sir Lintorn Simmons and his daughter's family, consisting of Blanch, Charles and Rotha, took rooms in Woodleigh Tower, a residential hotel in Bournemouth with views out to sea. Also lodging at the hotel were their servants, four in all including Florence Perry, Rotha's governess.[7]

Contemporary postcards with pictures of Woodleigh Tower Hotel show a rather fine, but small, hotel which features an hexagonal tower on one corner. The hotel was surrounded by well-maintained gardens, with walks where residents could take their ease. Advertising material of the time described the cuisine as 'excellent' and the terms as 'moderate' and all the rooms as having 'gas fires'.

After leaving Woodleigh Tower, Sir Lintorn took up residence at his Hampshire estate, Hawley House, while his daughter and son-in-law, with their daughter Rotha, moved to set up home at Morley House in Blackwater, adjacent to the Hawley House estate. During the period in which the Orman family, along with their grandfather, had been living at Woodleigh Tower, Sir Lintorn's other daughter Eleanor, half-sister to Blanch, was failing in health. She was a patient in hospital at Lansdown Grove in Bath,[8] more correctly a sanatorium for treating long term illnesses, from where she was later transferred to a smaller unit in the village of Walton-in-Gordano for what were to be her final months.

Eleanor Julia Lintorn Simmons passed away in October 1901 at Walton-in-Gordano with her death certificate indicating that her long term illness and cause of death was 'organic disease of the brain'.[9] Without any evidence to support such a claim, there must remain the possibility that her condition might be related to the fact that her parents, John Lintorn Simmons and Ellen Lintorn Simmons, were first cousins. The children of such marriages are sometimes the victims of mental illness or handicap, and this may explain her living away from her family in Somerset, while her parents were very much London orientated.

When Eleanor's will went to probate she left more than £26,000 for her executors to distribute, one of whom was Rotha's father.[10] According to a report in the *Clifton Society* the details of her will left a gift of £100 to Rotha, similar amounts to close family and friends but the residue, being the bulk of her estate, to William Alfred Moorart Dennison, a cousin and close friend from her childhood. £26,000 was a large sum of money and it can only be assumed that this represented an amount settled on her, or bequeathed to her at some stage.

Again the family travelled to Churchill in Somerset, this time for Eleanor's funeral and burial. Rotha was now six years old and a little more aware of the realities of life and death, but would have been well shielded from the harshness of mental illness and the stigma that went with it. The funeral service was in two parts, the first at Langford in the church that her father had financed only a year or two before, the second at the older family church of St John the Baptist in Churchill where she was finally laid to rest in the family plot.

There is clear evidence that people of that period were reluctant to admit to learning difficulties being discovered within the family, as borne out by the Fane and Bowes-Lyon families, each producing children that suffered mental illnesses. Henry Fane and John Bowes-Lyon had married sisters, Harriett and Fenella Trefusis, and although some children were born healthy, others were born with learning difficulties; these latter children were confined in asylums for their entire lives. John Bowes-Lyon was the brother of Elizabeth Bowes-Lyon, who went on to marry George VI, and she managed to keep the family secret into her old age.

The following summer saw plans being put in place for the coronation of Edward VII, Queen Victoria's eldest son. The ceremony had originally been planned for June 1902 but was put back to August when the king underwent an operation for appendicitis. The village of Hawley in Hampshire planned its own celebration, beginning with the planting of an English oak in the corner of the village green. This was ceremonially planted by Sir Lintorn Simmonds, being the occupant of the village's most prestigious property. Unfortunately the tree failed to grow, having to be replaced two years later. The second tree also failed to thrive, and it in turn was replaced by a third tree, but this time by a member of the maple family.

The coronation passed, and Rotha was then eight years old when the most significant change in her family life took place, simultaneously taking from her the undisputed head of the family, but also offering her the greatest opportunities for future personal freedom. Her grandfather, Sir Lintorn Simmons, died leaving her mother and father a legacy of wealth that could offer them all an unrestrained lifestyle, and the freedom to follow an unconventional path through the years between 1903 and 1914.

As Sir Lintorn Simmons had lain gravely ill reports of his decline were reported in various newspapers, describing him as being in a critical condition at home in Hawley House, with his family close by him. During the illness his eighty-second birthday passed without mention or celebration and his death was finally announced in the evening newspapers of 14 February 1903. The first part of the funeral was a rather formal military affair but the actual internment took place at St John the Baptist church in Churchill; described as a private ceremony, the *Western Daily Press* still reported the funeral as well attended by locals.

Flags were seen flying half-mast at many public and private buildings, a large congregation filled the church and hundreds more stood outside. The service was described as simple but impressive, the choir sang, the organist played and there was a muffled peal of the church bells. A large number of wreaths were in evidence, some from branches of the military, some from family friends. While the main funeral at Churchill was taking place there was a simultaneous memorial service taking place at St George's Garrison Church in Aldershot.

Sir Lintorn's death, at Hawley House, prompted a number of obituaries, particularly from the *Times* newspaper which mentioned his early education at Elizabeth College, Guernsey and then at the Royal Military Academy, Woolwich where he obtained his first commission as second lieutenant. His military duties took him to Canada, Constantinople, Silistra, Sevastopol and Warsaw. Outside his military duties he was appointed Governor of Malta and later Envoy Extraordinary and Minister Plenipotentiary to the Pope, a trip on which he had again been accompanied by Rotha's mother, prior to her marriage to Charles Orman.

An extract from *The History of the Corps of Royal Engineers* by Colonel Sir Charles M. Watson, written in 1914, describes his funeral and burial:

> He had left instructions that he desired to be buried at Churchill, in Somersetshire, beside his wife; but a military funeral, in accordance with his rank of Field Marshal, which was attended by a large number of troops from Aldershot, was held at Hawley Church by order of His Majesty the King. The King, the Prince of Wales, the German Emperor, and the Duke of Cambridge all sent representatives to the funeral, and the pall-bearers were some of his personal friends and officers who had been his aides-de-camp.[11]

As the funeral procession left Hawley House for Blackwater railway station for the journey to Churchill, the route was lined with troops, and an artillery battery sounded a minute-gun[12] salute. The funeral procession first stopped at the church in Langford before then proceeding to Churchill where, despite it being a private funeral, the service was conducted by the retired military Chaplain-General, rather than by a member of the local clergy. Blanch's function at the funeral was to carry Sir Lintorn's decorations and medals, in keeping with her role as chief mourner.

> There was a large gathering of people at Yatton Station last evening, when the body of the Field Marshal arrived there . . . the coffin was covered with wreaths and as soon

> as those present had entered the carriages the cortege moved away . . . the coffin was taken to Langford Church . . . where it remained during the night.[13]

At probate his estate was valued at over £20,000[14] his daughter Blanch Orman being named as executrix. With no other close family to inherit, Charles and Blanch were suddenly very wealthy people, with Blanch effectively holding the purse strings in the marriage. They were both of an age when adding further children to the family was unlikely so potentially, Rotha Beryl Lintorn Orman carrying the name Lintorn forward, was to eventually due to inherit a fortune from her parents.

It may be worth taking time to note that although Charles Orman was named as one of the executors for Eleanor Simmons, he was not named in Sir Lintorn Simmons will. It begs the question as to whether Charles was ever fully accepted into the Simmons family, but if not then why was he named as an executor of Eleanor's estate? In years yet to come it might be observed that Charles is somewhat excluded from matters concerning the Simmons estate, eventually separating from his wife, Blanch.

Meanwhile, in Switzerland, a young immigrant elementary school teacher arrived in Geneva to begin work as a stonemason in the city; a not entirely successful attempt at a new career. Leaving Geneva for Fribourg, and then Bern he finally gave up on being a stonemason and reverted to the more intellectual occupation of journalist on a socialist newspaper. He had originally left Italy for Switzerland in order to avoid compulsory military service, and so there would be charges hanging over him should he return to his homeland in the future. Benito Mussolini was to eventually reject socialism and embrace National Socialism, a step that would inspire Rotha to enter the world of politics.

In London's Mayfair a child, a little less than two years younger than Rotha, and loosely related to Elizabeth Bowes-Lyon was another budding politician. She was to become the wife of George VI, later known as the Queen Mother, and was to become the mother of Queen Elizabeth II. This young child was to move to live in Betton Hall near Market Drayton with his mother and paternal grandfather. Within the family he was always known as 'Tom' and attended West Downs School and Winchester College. In later years he would become her nemesis; his name was Oswald Moseley.

*Chapter 3*

## Forest Mere

Champneys Spa Resort at Forest Mere, just outside Liphook in Hampshire, lies in manicured grounds surrounding a tranquil lake, all within a woodland setting. On a summer afternoon small rowing boats drift across the water; along the paths and cycle tracks hotel guests take their leisure, and their exercise seriously – and expensively. To describe Champneys as exclusive would not be an overstatement; here come some of the most famous names in the country, and beyond, seeking relaxation and restoration.

The buildings are modern, light and airy. Glass and wood feature prominently in the design of the spa building; exercise and treatment rooms, swimming pools, restaurants and kitchens. All these modern buildings are constructed around one central architectural feature, that being the original house built by Sir Henry Cotton in the 1880s. The house was originally named Folly but later Forest Mere, the name it went by when Charles Edward Orman purchased a thirteen-year lease on the estate in 1904. While Charles was not a poor man, the purchase of the Forest Mere lease was only possible following his wife Blanch inheriting a substantial sum from her father, Field Marshal Sir John Lintorn Arabin Simmons.

With Blanch's half-sister Eleanor having died before Sir Lintorn, the entire estate had now passed to his only surviving daughter and thus, in effect, to the Orman family. The Hawley estate that Sir Lintorn Simmons had called home, was really too large for that young family to take on, and just how to pay taxes on the estate would require some serious thought. The Somerset estate was too precious to the Simmons family, now the Orman family, to sell and Blanch Orman kept a very close hand on the financial management of her legacy. Later events would demonstrate that she and her husband were not entirely agreed on how best to exercise that joint responsibility.

The Forest Mere house was built in a style typical of Sussex and Hampshire, the ground floor of stone and brick and the upper floors hung with pan-tiles, highly decorative and reflecting the gentle sunlight to provide a warm glow to the onlooker. The steep pitched roof provided additional rooms looking out over the twenty acres of Folly Lake, with its small island at the centre. When Forest Mere was previously auctioned in 1894 it had been described as having 'pretty pleasure grounds, productive kitchen gardens and numerous glass-houses'. At that time the entire estate ran to over 650 acres, but had been somewhat reduced in size by the time the Orman family took up residence.

Charles, Blanch and their daughter Rotha had moved from Morley House in Blackwater, part of the Hawley House estate, the home of Rotha's maternal grandfather. Before that, the entire family had briefly lived at Woodleigh Tower in Bournemouth, where they employed a governess for Rotha as well as two domestic servants. At this new, more prestigious, residence they employed a governess and four domestic servants, as well as other staff, including two chauffeurs and a valet; the staff total coming to eleven. Charles Orman's elderly mother and a young girl by the name of Nesta Maude, a companion for Rotha, made up the household. Mrs Orman senior was not resident at Forest Mere for very long, having decided to return to Bedfordshire where she had made her home lately with her son John Julius Orman.

The two girls each had their own personal maid and were indulged with their own ponies and dogs. Rotha and Nesta were to travel together with the Orman family, to Europe and beyond.[1] The commentary on these early years comes from a book, largely autobiographical, written by Nesta Maude, later Nesta Ashworth, and posthumously edited by her daughters Mary Ashworth and Margaret Spencer. In later years, Rotha seems to have contradicted all the expected trappings of a feminine nature and adopted a more masculine dress and disposition. Even so, in reading Nesta Maude's description of her, there is nothing to suggest that these later traits, either in behaviour or dress, were in evidence while she was in her formative years. Indeed the young Rotha appears to have been quite content in her embroidered silk evening and dance dresses, her liberty bodices and her stockings and suspenders.

Before joining the Orman household Nesta Maude had been living in Crowborough in East Sussex with her father and mother. Ronald, her younger brother, was working for the Deasy Motorcar Manufacturing Company in Coventry and was tasked, with two colleagues, to deliver a pair of motorcars to Charles Orman at Forest Mere, a process that took some days for the 'handover' to be completed. The role of the chauffeur was very different in the early days of the twentieth century than it is today; not only that of a driver, but also an engineer, having to be schooled in the idiosyncrasies of each new model and then being able to carry out necessary repairs.

The purchase of two motor cars is an indication of just how wealthy the Orman family was, now they had Sir Lintorn's inheritance. The two motor cars were each powered by a four cylinder water-cooled engine producing about twelve horsepower, with the coachwork finished in a rather conservative green. Even by the standards of the day, such a purchase might be considered as extravagant and something of a self-indulgence. In the eyes of Charles Orman it was an indication of his station in life. He was now a man of means, bathing in reflected glory, and wealth.

The two motor cars may be an indication of Charles' new found wealth; one was identified as a 'touring' car by Nesta, so the other might have been somewhat more formal. This would explain them owning two motor cars; different outings, different vehicles. Two chauffeurs however, for such a small family, suggests the Charles and Blanch led two different lives and so travelled separately on multiple occasions; perhaps not as close as many couples.

The two Deasy engineers were meant to be staying with the two chauffeurs from the household but, with Ronald being sent to accompany them as part of his training, there was insufficient room and so Blanch Orman invited Ronald Maude to stay in the main house with the family. Very soon after arriving he was playing tennis, swimming and fishing with thirteen-year-old Rotha, and gradually becoming an integral part of the household. He described his own family background to Blanch

Orman, the outcome being that an invitation was extended to Ronald's sister Nesta, to come and spend two weeks of her school holiday at Forest Mere, as Rotha's companion.

It is interesting to speculate why the young man, Ronald Maude, was included within the Orman household during that visit. Nesta Maude gives very little information other than saying 'Arrangements . . . embarrassed, and arrangements were altered and Ronald joined the Orman family and was soon swimming and fishing with the Orman's fourteen-year-old daughter, Rotha'. It's possible that Blanch saw something lacking in Rotha's childhood and recognised the value that companionship brought to her daughter.

Companionship for Rotha, however exalted, could be no substitute for the friendship that she could gain from having a confidant, somebody to share her secrets with, someone to be part of Rotha's world rather than she be part of theirs, a friend who would be a buffer against the adults in an adult world. This transition was not an easy one for Nesta to make, her own comments on the difficulties also throw some light on the Orman lifestyle.

> I had never had to help myself from silver dishes handed over my left shoulder, and as dinner every night consisted of soup, fish, an entree, and a main dish, sweet, savoury, and dessert, the array of cutlery put me in a panic.[2]

A further insight is gained by the fact that Nesta is particularly grateful that neither Blanch nor Charles ever showed her anything but kindness, and certainly gave no sign of noticing her social awkwardness. Indeed Nesta, in her autobiography, never has a single word to say about Blanch, Charles or Rotha that is other than complimentary.

Nesta mentions, in her autobiography, that the Ormans, and Sir Lintorn before his death, took a particular interest in the Gordon Boys' Home and that they had youngsters at Forest Mere to be trained for domestic service in large establishments; learning to wait at table, clean silver, announce visitors etc. According to Nesta, the lady of the house kept in touch with many of the boys long after they had left Forest Mere and were making their way in the world. The Boy's Home was run on military lines, in keeping with its namesake, General Gordon of Khartoum of whom Sir Lintorn had been a close personal friend, and many of the boys who made the decision not to go into service would make their career in the army or navy.

Sir Lintorn had not simply been a friend of General Gordon, but was also chairman of the Gordon Boys' Home charitable trust. The patron of the trust had been Queen Victoria, but was at this time King Edward VII, the patronage having passed down from monarch to monarch. In recognition of his standing, a memorial to Sir Lintorn was erected at the Gordon Boys' Home in Woking, which is today a state secondary school with academy status, educating girls as well as boys.

Before the two weeks were concluded Blanch Orman confided in the young Nesta that she would like her to stay with the family for a year or so, as a companion to Rotha, and to share lessons from the shortly to be engaged governess. Rotha claimed the idea had originally been solely hers, rather than her mother's, but clearly she and Nesta were both enthusiastic at the prospect. It's not clear what the process was in obtaining the agreement of Mr and Mrs Maude for the transition as Nesta's parents had recently moved to Switzerland because Mr Maud's health was giving some cause for concern, leaving Nesta boarding at a local school in Sussex. Nesta did not make the return trip to Crowborough before she took up permanent residence at Forest Mere.

Charles and Blanch were quite aristocratic in their lifestyle, one that Rotha took to quite naturally. There were clothes buying visits to London, where Blanch and the two girls stayed at the Savoy Hotel while on shopping trips to the Burlington Arcade and the other retail temples of the rich. According to Nesta, the self-confidence with which Rotha conducted herself in such a rarified atmosphere was quite amazing. Such confidence, as Nesta wrote, was entirely understandable for a young girl who was accustomed to playing with the children of the then Prince of Wales, now George V, and had met some of the most influential military men in the country through her grandfather, a man who had been given the accolade of Queen Victoria's favourite Field Marshal.

Despite this familiarity with the upper echelons of British society, Blanch Orman displayed a genuinely charitable side to her character. Having made the commitment to treat Nesta as an equal member of the family, her generosity was without limits. Nesta's wardrobe was of the same range and quality as Rotha's; warm underclothes and sweaters as well as ski outfits, evening dresses and dance dresses. Added to her wardrobe were schoolroom clothes of navy skirts and white Viyella blouses,[3] in anticipation of Miss Knox-Coffer's imminent arrival to become their new governess.

Rotha and her companion, Nesta, seemed to have shown an early interest in the outdoor pursuits that would guide them both through their next few years, and in Nesta's case through her whole life. The lake was a draw to the girls and they persuaded Mrs Pendergast, the housekeeper at Forest Mere, to provide them with an old sheet to use as a sail on the family's gig.[4] Blanch Orman, aware of the plan, adopted an attitude very similar to that to be later reflected in the character of Mrs Walker in the 1930 children's novel *Swallows and Amazons,* recommending to the girls that 'If you must fall overboard, try to avoid the muddy patch at the end of the lake'.[5]

The summer of 1908, when Rotha was thirteen years old, she and Nesta spent the days swimming, sailing, fishing and roaming through the fields and woods of the Forest Mere estate. It was in their joint enjoyment of the open air life that Rotha was able to learn from Nesta who, unlike Rotha, had been accustomed to a rural life in Crowborough rather than a sophisticated existence in the manicured gardens of Kensington, and was used to holidaying at the cold English seaside rather than luxuriating on a warm Mediterranean cruise.

As autumn brought the shorter days, indoor schoolwork was taken up again in earnest, and outdoor activities were confined to walks across the heath with the two dogs. The village of Milland was a little more than two miles walk from Forest Mere, and it was to Milland Vicarage that Rotha and Nesta walked each Saturday morning during autumn; this was the home of the Rev Frederick Charles Bland, who had his living from the parish.

Charles and Blanch Orman favoured a High Church form of Anglican worship but were flexible in their attendance. Years of military service, and frequent travel, had taught them that they should be content with any church service available, rather than non-adherence to their routine of Sunday worship. There was a beautiful chapel under the main staircase at Forest Mere, where prayers were read every morning for the entire household should they want it, but attendance for family, visitors and staff was entirely a matter of personal preference. Charles and Blanch were, as Nesta wrote 'tolerant and understanding of other Christians whose chosen way of worship was different from the service of their personal choice.'

The weekly visits to the Rev. Bland were in order to attend confirmation classes in preparation for the ceremony to be performed in November 1908. It was not only Rotha and Nesta who attended; other girls from the surrounding area were also part of the cohort and they all contributed to generating a sense of camaraderie that was to bear fruit during the coming weeks and months, and in Nesta's, case, a lifetime. Confirmation was to be performed by the Rt. Rev. William Awdry,[6] Bishop of South Tokyo, who had recently returned to the United Kingdom for his retirement.

It was customary for young people to receive gifts to celebrate their confirmation day; such gifts included prayer books, hymn books etc., as well as other non-religious items. One such non-religious item was given to Nesta by her older brother who, as a journalist had been given a copy of a book and asked to review it, a book that he had read on the train down from London. It was a paperback, somewhat grubby and dog-eared, and which was now of no further interest to him. Its title was *Scouting for Boys* by Lord Baden-Powell, and its contents were avidly received by both Nesta and Rotha, the girls devouring every word, much of it whilst sitting on the small island in the middle of Folly Lake.

This dog-eared book was, in fact, a revision of an earlier publication by Baden-Powell entitled *Aids to Scouting for NCOs and Men*, written in 1899, just prior to the siege of Mafeking. In his book he emphasised the need for pluck, self-reliance and discretion, also reminding soldiers that in preparation for their role in time of war they should practise their skills in peacetime. He emphasised that such men were selected for their 'grit' and were trained for one class of work only; reconnaissance, requiring them to use observation to follow tracks and to conceal themselves from the enemy. Far from being confined to the military, *Aids to Scouting for NCOs and Men* had sold more than 100,000 copies to the public by the time that Baden-Powell returned to the United Kingdom in 1903.

The audience for the book was largely young people fired by a sense of adventure, or youth leaders and schoolteachers attempting to instil such a sense in their young charges. It was mostly as a result of the interest shown in his book that prompted Baden-Powell to organise a prototype scout camp on Brownsea Island in Poole Harbour, attracting eleven boys from public schools and ten from state schools; Baden-Powell's nephew was also included in that number.

The choice of Brownsea was not by chance as Baden-Powell had visited Brownsea Island when a boy, and it was a location which provided insulation from press attention. The boys camped in military style bell-tents and the entire camp was run in line with a strict military etiquette. The camp, which lasted a week, operated to Baden-Powell's satisfaction and provided him with verification for the ideas that he was developing into this new book *Scouting for Boys*.

Baden-Powell's book fired the imagination of the two girls and their enthusiasm became the driving force for their free time. They read and studied *Scouting for Boys* from cover to cover, and where they needed outside information or techniques they sought it where they could. The second chauffeur did have tasks other than just driving and taking care of the motorcars, among his other duties was that of maintaining the electric generator to provide light for the house. More valuable to Rotha and Nesta however was the fact that he was an old sailor and they soon persuaded him to share his vast knowledge of rope and knots and all things practical; including almost certainly engines and motorcars.

There are elements within *Scouting for Boys* that had a direct bearing on Rotha's later life, the attitudes that she would adopt and the paths that she would follow.

> Other nations could formerly only look on and wonder, but now they too are pressing forward in the race for empire and commerce, so that we cannot afford to sit still or let things slide. We have had this enormous Empire handed down to us by our forefathers, and we

> are responsible that it develops and goes ahead . . . if we don't do this some other nation will take it from us . . . The surest way to keep peace is to be prepared for war . . . don't be cowards . . . do something in your own self-defence . . . learning how to shoot and to drill, to take his share in defence of the Empire . . . your forefathers worked hard, fought hard, and died hard, to make this Empire for you. Don't let them look down from heaven, and see you loafing about with hands in your pockets, doing nothing to keep it up.[7]

During these final years of the first decade of the century, tensions between Britain and Germany were increasing. There was certainly something of an arms war going on. Britain launched HMS *Dreadnought* in 1906, a battleship which fuelled a naval arms race as the Imperial German Navy rushed to match it in the building up of their own navy. Even civilian ships were seen as part of the buildup, the *Lusitania* built for Cunard having a potential troop transport role.

The tensions building between Britain and Germany were in political and military fields, with little or no effect on the ordinary citizen. There was a degree of free travel between the two countries, both for holidays and for business, and the long term relationship was only seen as the stronger for the royal family connections. Certainly the tensions were present within the diplomatic services but these were private or even secret.

The tensions developing in Russia were more to do with internal discontent than with militaristic expansion. The workers were threatening revolution and the rise of socialism was a worry to the western countries and their ruling aristocracy. The threat of the established order being overthrown, and a domino effect spreading to Britain and its empire, would undermine the very fabric of British society as it was known at this time.

Charles Orman was not an obvious political player but the same could not be said of Blanch Orman who moved within the highest levels of society. Rotha, her daughter, more aligned with her mother than her father, was at an impressionable age and open to persuasion. Her connection with the scouts reinforced her love of king and empire and no doubt influenced her early thinking.

*Chapter 4*

# Crystal Palace

The 1907 experiment for boys was not an entirely novel idea but was a consequence of Baden-Powell's experiences during the defence of Mafeking, when young boys were used as messengers during the siege. The enthusiasm and resourcefulness of the youngsters impressed him and he formed ideas for a new, adventure based, youth movement upon his return to Britain, but his plans had not taken into account the effect his writings would have on girls, as well as boys. Two girls so affected were already leading an outdoor scouting life, when they could escape their indoor studies, at Forest Mere.

Rotha and Nesta were fired with the idea of building a hut, as is described in Nesta's autobiography, and decided that the island, with its single tree, offered the ideal location. The Forest Mere estate provided an excellent source of building materials and, with their pocket money to finance the purchase of a hand axe, they searched the estate to find wood poles to form a framework, and dry heather for thatching. Having built their hut they then constructed a fireplace and a landing stage, inviting visitors from the 'house' to examine and pass judgement on their project.

Following the hut building adventure the family, including Nesta, travelled to Switzerland for a winter sports holiday. Nesta makes no mention of visiting her parent, who are assumed to be still living in that country. As a matter of interest she never mentions her parents in the whole autobiography, except in relation to her returning after her education, although she does use the word 'hardly', implying limited contact at least.

> About three weeks before Christmas 1912, I went back to Crowborough to settle down to a home life with parents I had seen very little of for over five years, two brothers I had hardly at all . . . it was funny to be clearing the table, washing the silver, and dusting the furniture . . .[1]

Rotha was described as being quite a fair skier and, although the girls enjoyed the slopes, they appear also to have succumbed to the charms of two young naval cadets, and spent the greater part of the holiday as a foursome, with much dancing. Nesta Maude offers here a description of Rotha Orman which shows little similarity to her later indications of masculinity. Both in her manner and choice of evening and dance dresses, made from Swiss silk decorated with edelweiss, and her sexual preference for young, good looking men in uniform, suggests otherwise.

The winter sports holiday over, the family returned to Forest Mere, and the two girls' attention returned to schoolwork and everyday things, but above all to *Scouting for Boys* and the prospect of joining with others from outside the Forest Mere estate. Baden-Powell's book had raised an interest among the youth of the country but, as yet, had not built a structure which could properly develop into a movement. Here was a situation which was due to be remedied; there was a rumour that change was in the air and that Baden-Powell was about to do something that would bring such a movement into being.

Rotha and Nesta were, by now, taking a weekly newspaper named *The Scout*, not published by Baden-Powell himself but by his friend and newspaper publisher Cyril Arthur Pearson. It was in reading *The Scout* they first became aware that girls were not going to be allowed to enrol in the new Baden-Powell movement which had been formed as result of the Brownsea Island experiment. Their solution was simple; to present themselves as androgynous, using the initials R and N, rather than the names Rotha and Nesta, thus allowing Scout Headquarters to draw their own conclusion that they were dealing with boys. Although Rotha and Nesta were not in touch with any other like-minded girls, it seems that a similar thought had occurred across the country and that a number of girls had come to the same conclusion.

Although there were formalities for boys, or girls, to become a scout and join the new movement, it seems there were no hurdles to be surmounted in the case of the Scout Master, or Scout Mistress, no gender qualification was prescribed nor implied in those early days. This was most probably because adult leadership was thought to be necessary and that mothers were more likely to put themselves forward for this role than were fathers.

Here we see that Blanch is unable to occupy the role of a supporter of Rotha, but must be an integral part of her hobby or pastime. She procures for her daughter the companionship she needs, in the form of Nesta, yet is unable to let Rotha pursue her and Nesta's interest without having to become involved in that interest; not only a participant, but a senior 'officer' guiding them on their way.

Blanch Orman was very supportive of the two girls and consented to be Scout Mistress of a Forest Mere Troop which would consist of two patrol leaders, Rotha and Nesta, and a dozen or more recruits drawn from the locality. The 'tenderfoots' were instructed by the two patrol leaders in semaphore, camping, fire-lighting, outdoor cooking, first aid and some knot-tying.

> We divided the training between us fairly evenly. I took the First Aid and signalling and nature while Rotha had all the drills and camp crafts such as tracking, fires, hut building, and so on. I tried always to make my First Aid accidents look as real as possible and sometimes I would leave it to one girl to stage an emergency that had to be diagnosed and treated by the other patrol. On one occasion a girl managed to stick a little bit of bone to her shin surrounded by a little scarlet grease paint. This was greeted by shrieks of delight and the information that it was a 'constipated fracture'.[2]

In the spring of 1909 there was a plan to camp at Forest Mere for a week, on what was by now referred to as One Tree Island, living off the land and lake as much as was possible, although they did agree to take a sufficient supply of tinned essentials with them. The camp was entirely successful but just for the two patrol leaders; the rank and file stayed at home, preferring to remain comfortable and well fed! Rotha and Nesta managed to survive the week, living on rabbits from the estate and fish from the lake; it was on their return that they realised they had not taken a tin opener.

The question of girls being involved with the scouting movement came to a head in the autumn of 1909, when Baden-Powell organised the first national Rally for Scouts. This was to be held at the Crystal Palace in London with a potential attendance of between 500 and 2,000 boys. In fact 10,000 boys turned up in full uniform, with one troop from Scotland sporting kilts. Saturday 4 September was cold, windy and drizzling with rain, but the boys were able to sing and whistle according to the Scout Law's instruction. Rotha and Nesta, despite their gender, were driven to the Crystal Palace by Blanch, clutching their Scout membership cards. They were stopped at the gate and told that they could not join the rally but that they should simply sit in the stands and watch.

Entrance to the Rally was simply enough achieved by attaching themselves to a troop of boys and staying on the blind side of the gate marshal until well inside, a practice also followed by many other girls in a similar predicament. The girls appeared, while masked by a crowd of boys, to be in regular uniform including the broad brimmed hat, except that on closer inspection they were seen to sport ankle length skirts instead of shorts. Having achieved entry they were then at a loss as to how to proceed.

According to Nesta's narrative, there were girls at the Rally, but calling themselves by other names than Girl Scouts. The most numerous were the Girls Emergency Corps, which was the initiative of Baden-Powell's sister Agnes who had formed that organisation in 1908.[3] These girls marched at the rear of the column and numbered about 2,000, bringing the total number of attendees to around 12,000 young people. Rotha and Nesta, who had arrived purely in hope of marching, could only stand and watch. The two were part of this non-aligned contingent of girls who coalesced around Rotha; when Baden-Powell asked 'Who are you?' and Rotha replied 'We're the Girl Scouts'.

This account is slightly at odds with the account given elsewhere which claims that Baden-Powell had been aware of girls joining the movement from the very start. A letter from Baden-Powell, dated 28 March 1908 reads 'I am glad to hear you are taking up scouting. I think there can be girl scouts just as well as boy scouts, and hope you will form a patrol, and let us know as yours will be the first girl scout patrol.'

Whatever the truth of that somewhat apocryphal exchange, the inclusion of girls into the Scouting movement followed fairly soon after. There were several references to Girl Scouts in subsequent editions of *The Scout* including Baden-Powell describing a scheme for Girl Guides with a detailed description of uniform, proficiency badges and rules for girls to be admitted into the Order of the Silver Fish, the highest award in guiding. Agnes Baden-Powell reluctantly agreed to head the new movement and on 31 May 1910 the Girl Guides became a separate organisation from the Boy Scouts.[4]

Nesta, writing about the sentiments that she and Rotha shared, was not entirely happy with the change of name, nor with control passing from the adventurous Robert Baden-Powell to his more staid and homely sister. Where he had been the 'Chief' she was the 'President', a more suitable title, thought Nesta, for the leader of the YWCA or of a local flower show; there seemed little capacity for the unmarried Agnes to appreciate the feelings and ambitions of a generation of what were to become young ‘flappers’.

When a letter arrived at Forest Mere, addressed to the two patrol leaders, with a request to attend Agnes at her house in Forest Gate, they were a little surprised by the invitation, but this probably had more to do with Rotha’s, or at least Blanche’s, social connections rather than the quality of the two girls’ opinions. The girls were driven to their afternoon tea appointment with the President and told that they would be picked up again in one and a half hours. They were admitted and shown upstairs to meet their hostess.

What the girls did not appreciate was that they had not been invited for an intimate chat with Agnes alone, but for an interrogation by the ladies of the committee. The ladies asked about sewing and cooking, health rules and personal hygiene, whether they took their troop on nature walks and whether they organised picnics. No mention of tracking, lighting fires or of camping. Efforts by Rotha and Nesta to include such topics in the conversation resulted in the caution that it was a girls’ movement and that they must resist the temptation to emulate the boys. Rotha’s whispered comment to Nesta, upon leaving the gathering, was that the ladies of the committee ‘made the boys sound slimy, and a little like slugs’.

The high spot of the day for them came with the unexpected arrival of Robert Baden-Powell himself into the room. He shook hands with the ladies and returned the Scout salute from the girls. He exchanged a couple of pleasantries with Rotha and Nesta, gave a little bow to the assembled company, and left the gathering. Nesta makes no further mention of Agnes and her committee of worthy ladies, nor of the transition from Girl Scouts to Girl Guides, nor any mention of Blanch in this transformation.

The two girls were approaching the age when an end to their formal education was in sight. In 1910 the Orman family made a trip to Oberammergau in order to see the famous Passion Play that commemorated the passing of the bubonic plague from that German village in 1634. They made the journey by road via Ostend, Rheims and Munich before reaching their final destination. In the Bavarian alps. Rotha and Nesta, although under age, could both drive and were familiar with the technical and mechanical terms in a number of European languages. The two girls both secretly hoped that Judd the chauffeur would find himself unable to drive the whole way to and from Bavaria, but were to be disappointed in that. Rotha's love of the motorcar would surely manifest itself in her later calling towards vehicles and driving.

Nesta gives some insight as to the characters of Charles and Blanch Orman when she describes them both as having 'such pleasant manners and the happy knack of expecting the best service and therefore getting it and willing to pay for it'. She also mentions that Blanch was fluent in French and German, and that the chauffeur also had a working knowledge of Dutch, and so they fared pretty well.

Once they reached the village of Oberammergau, Rotha and Nesta played a small part in the presentation of the Passion Play, their responsibility being to collect the donkey from its paddock each morning, and ensure that it was saddled and waiting for the actor who was playing Jesus to ride in for the Palm Sunday scene of the play. The girls seemed to strike up a particular rapport with Lang, the actor playing the part of Jesus that year, and his young family.

Charles and Blanch Orman had obviously stayed with Anton Lang and his family on previous visits to Germany and were already known in the village. On their return from Bavaria, two young women, with whom Rotha and Nesta had made friends, also travelled with the Ormans, in order for them to join the staff at Forest Mere and so improve their English.

The last summer that the two girls were together they camped in the Lake District, hiring a Romany caravan drawn by a carthorse that went by the name of Briton, guaranteed to be quiet and strong. Four others completed the group of six young women that planned to camp, four walking the route, the other two riding, on a rotating schedule. During that trip the group was fortunate enough to encounter a real accident involving a coach party of ladies in need of assistance, having been thrown onto the road by a collision with a hay cart.

This, of course, was exactly what these Guides had been hoping for, there was satisfaction in knowing that their years of training had use in the real world, where blood was messy, patients were frightened and in pain, and the girls could fulfil the purpose for which they were intended. At that moment theirs was the cool voice of reason, a role that Rotha would adopt in later life, both in wartime and in peacetime; both in the face of a real enemy and in the face of an imagined one.

There were cuts and bruises, the injured taking shelter in the local vicar's garden, where the girls were assisted by the vicar's son. Word was sent to Keswick and motor transport arrived to take the injured to hospital. Following the accident the group of girls spent some time in the neighbourhood, making several return visits to the vicarage. Once they departed, they were often visited en route by the vicar's son, riding a bicycle. A relationship blossomed, and in 1920 Nesta and the vicar's son were married.

The position of Blanch within the scout and guide movement, and the Forest Mere troop, is still something of mystery; the three operated as a triumvirate, living by their own rules, even to the point of Blanch driving them to the Crystal Palace under false pretences. Although the threesome expressed a desire to be part of a larger whole, they seemed to be more content as mavericks in a masculine world, borne out by their unhappiness in becoming Girl Guides, and their never getting round to appointing a third patrol leader.

One interesting point to come out of these preceding accounts of Rotha's early years is just how close she is to her mother, almost to the exclusion of all others. Charles Orman appears to make little impression upon Nesta, he seems to have lived his life separately from his family, although she says nothing that could be considered as being critical of him. Blanch appears to gather her small brood around her, including Nesta, and is content with that close circle. Even Rotha's enthusiasm for scouting is usurped by her mother, who places herself 'front and centre' in the movement, but slightly superior to her daughter in the hierarchy.

Rotha does not appear to have held any disdain for the male sex, in fact at fourteen she was quite scathing that the ladies gathered around Baden-Powell's sister Agnes should speak of 'boys' as though it was 'not a very nice word' and made them 'sound a bit slimy, like slugs'. It's all too easy to interpret her natural frustration with the Victorian standards of behaviour and deportment that were expected of her as exhibiting traits of masculinity. We would not interpret the behaviour of a young girl in the twenty-first century who played football or rugby, ran marathons or threw the javelin, rowed or white water rafted, as being abnormal - she would be considered as modern and progressive, and a credit to her sex.

At the end of 1912 life for the family changed dramatically. It marked the departure of their governess, Lily Knox-Cotter, and of Nesta's return home to her family in Crowborough where she was almost a stranger after nearly five years away. Before the girls parted they were treated to private dancing lessons and attended a number of local dances. Again, there is nothing to indicate that Rotha was anything but delighted with her 'fun year' and what Nesta described as completing 'the growing up process'.

Charles Orman's lease on Forest Mere expired at the end of 1912 and the Orman family moved to a smaller home in Christchurch Road, Bournemouth, where Rotha and her mother further developed their interest in the Boy Scout and Girl Guide movements. Nesta went on to spend a lifetime with the Girl Guides. During the the First World War the leader of the Sunflowers Patrol, Nesta, joined the Mechanical Transport Section of the Royal Flying Corps, and then in the Second

World War worked with the WVS in London, finally emigrating to British Columbia where she and her husband lived out the remainder of their lives.

At the end of December 1912 an announcement appeared in the *Bedfordshire Times* in which Charles Orman gave notice that he had changed his name, and that of his family, by deed poll to Lintorn-Orman and that he would be known by that name henceforth. This was obviously in consideration of the legacy that he and Blanch had received from her father, although the purpose behind the change can only be guessed at. It might have been an effort to placate Blanch in some way, Charles feeling a little insecure. The change of name caused one small anomaly in that Rotha Beryl Lintorn Orman now became Rotha Beryl Lintorn Lintorn-Orman; she dropped the first Lintorn.

The choice of Bedfordshire to make the announcement of a name change might seem strange, but it could be explained by the fact that Charles' mother, Isabella, and two daughters had recently moved to 'Swallowfield' at 10 Bushmead Avenue in Bedford. The rather remote Bedfordshire location, rather than a more usual London one, might indicate that all was not well within the Orman/Simmons household. Charles' immediate family, mother, sisters and brother were now all living in the county, leaving Charles somewhat isolated.

Life at 68 Christchurch Road, Bournemouth was a far cry from the Forest Mere existence that Rotha had enjoyed during the previous thirteen years. The house, on the corner of Chichester Road and Knyveton Road, was named 'Hawley Grange', supposedly after the village in which Sir Lintorn

Simmons had his Hampshire residence. Other than it being large enough to contain the trappings of wealth in keeping with the name Lintorn-Orman, their new home was hardly splendid, but did provide a base from which Blanch could undertake her various projects.

Rotha's interest in Guiding continued and she is credited with forming a new Girl Guide troop in Bournemouth, 1st Bournemouth Company. In 1913 Rotha was asked to organise the Girl Guide contribution to the Children's Welfare Exhibition at Olympia. Originally both she and Nesta had been asked but Nesta, Crowborough based, now limited her involvement to taking charge of the Forest Mere Company, that happened to be attending the exhibition. This occasion was probably the last time that Rotha and Nesta were together as girlhood friends, although when Nesta's mother died in 1914, Charles, Blanch and Rotha attended her funeral in Crowborough.

During the last few years before the war, Rotha's mother dedicated her time to ensuring that her daughter acquired some of the attributes that a young woman of her position in society demanded. Dance lessons were a vital component, as was behaving comfortably in the highest society, to which ends visits were made to the Empress Eugenie for Rotha to gain experience. She attended dances at the Royal Military College and those held in private houses, which were quite permissible for a girl of her age.

During the period, and up to 1914, votes for women had become a major issue, including the militant group that went by the name 'suffragettes', first coined in 1906 by the *Daily*

*Mail*, as a term of abuse. The women embraced that name and adopted it as the name of their journal. These women were to play an increasing role in Rotha's life, as she fell under their spell during the war years, and gained their support during her political life.

Rotha's role in the Girl Guides might have some bearing on her later life and attitudes. While Nesta might be seen to have displayed a more caring approach, both nursing and pastoral teaching being her strength, Rotha might be seen as more interested in the organisation, uniform and drilling of the troop. One small indication of how the two patrol leaders were perceived by their younger members was from an encounter between Nesta and one of the Troop, some fifty years later. She was told that while she was known as 'Lovable Bear' by her patrol, Rotha was known as 'Tiger' by hers.

Having left Forest Mere for Bournemouth, Blanch Lintorn-Orman was still very active in the movement, holding the position of Girl Guide Commissioner for Hampshire, Poole and Parkstone. She attended many Girl Guide events across the region, often accompanied by Rotha, who generally played a part in the proceedings. Rotha's father also gains a mention from time to time, the Bournemouth Troop, having its headquarters at Hawley Grange, but generally appears to have been less and less involved.

Meanwhile, away from the 'man in the street' tensions in Europe were building. Positions taken by the European nations were becoming firm, and political leaders more entrenched, such that the slightest spark could set Europe ablaze. Eventually the tensions began to mount, first in government corridors and then in the streets. Volunteer groups began to be organised, funds for defence and funds to relieve suffering, the suspension of campaigns that may be seen as unpatriotic, and the desire to stand back from Europe and for the country to enjoy its splendid isolation.

*Chapter 5*

# The Ambulance Corps

The First World War began on 28 July 1914, triggered by the death of Archduke Franz Ferdinand in Sarajevo, the victim of a Serbian assassin. That is not to say that the assassination was the cause of the war, but it was the spark that initiated the chain reaction which led to all-out war. A month after the assassination, troops of the Austro-Hungarian Alliance declared war on Serbia which, in turn, brought Russia into the war to defend its ally. As a consequence, France entered the war as part of the 1892 Secret Treaty with Russia, causing Germany to initiate their Schlieffen Plan, which included the German invasion of Belgium, in turn bringing Great Britain into the conflict.

> Instead of aiming the first strike against Russia, the 'Schlieffen Plan' called for a decisive debilitating blow at France through Belgium, rather than directly across the heavily fortified border between Germany and France. This plan was based upon the assumption that Russia would take six weeks in order to fully mobilise, and that, during such period, Germany could deliver a devastating blow to France before then turning east and facing Russia.[1]

In less than three months, an isolated act of foolishness by Gavrilo Princip, a nineteen-year-old student in Serbia, had led to Germany's invasion of France, and the British Expeditionary Force being bogged down in protracted trench warfare. The resultant patriotic wave of emotion that flooded across Britain was almost palpable, manifesting itself in young men wanting to join the army and fight, young ladies wanting to nurse, old soldiers expounding on their battle plans and old ladies forming committees. For the average working class man or woman in the street it simply meant work; in the factories, in the mines and in the fields.

There had been disquiet in the Balkans for a number of years prior to the First World War, particularly with the occupation of land by Austria-Hungary and the resultant political manoeuvring by the Russian empire. The Balkan wars ended with the Treaty of London, reducing the size of the Ottoman Empire, only for Serbia and Greece to be invaded by Austria-Hungary, which drew Russia into the dispute.

The plight of Serbia garnered a wave of sympathy in Britain, particularly as that country was already suffering from its previous conflicts and was depleted of both men and machines, as well as being in financial difficulties with a shortage of food in prospect. The Serbian forces were outnumbered by nearly 3:2 and were no match for the aggressors. It was at this stage that many of the young suffrage campaigners who were about to be 'stood down' took up the cause of Serbia. By December 1914 the call had been answered with Evelina Haverfield at its head.

> Not many days ago the National Union of Women's Suffrage Societies sent off its first women's unit for service in France. Now a second contingent has started for Serbia . . . Amongst those who were there to bid them farewell was . . . Dr Elsie Ingles, the organiser of the hospitals . . . The unit is composed entirely of women, with the exception of two men who have volunteered as orderlies.[2]

The response to Britain declaring war on Germany was overwhelming in its support by the general population. The whole country was at one with the sentiment of 'Poor little Belgium' being invaded by Germany and it being Britain's duty to honour the terms of the 1839 Treaty of London, which guaranteed Belgium's independence and neutrality. The British mobilised an expeditionary force, which met the German army at Mons, and then dug in to a form of trench warfare, which dictated the direction of the war on the western front.

Political dissent in Britain was paused, or at least tempered, with the outbreak of war. Both Rotha and her mother Blanch, now Lintorn-Orman rather than just plain Orman, had been supporters of Women's Suffrage, although there is no indication that they were particularly active within the movement, certainly no indication of militancy. The Pankhurst led Women's Social and Political Union (WSPU) turned its attention to patriotism, changed the name of its newspaper from the *Suffragette* to the *Britannia*, and was rewarded with the release of all Suffragette prisoners. Some of their members were unhappy with the suspension of the campaign and with their being asked to give support to what they saw as a hostile government, but this was far from being a universal reaction.

The obvious parallels to be drawn between the militant activities of the Suffrage movement, and the consequences of the country being at war with Germany, would have caused a dilemma for young women of the Women's Social and Political Union (WSPU), the motto of which was 'deeds, not words'. Emmeline Pankhurst avoided the possibility of that confliction by suspending all militancy at the outbreak of war, although peaceful protest continued throughout the war years.

With no formal leadership or backing, the movement could not continue as a militant force, and offered no prospect of a renewal while the war continued. The mood of the country was such that any militancy could be easily used by opponents to imply disloyalty, even treason. Such a label being applied to the movement for women's suffrage could well destroy any hopes of success when the war was ended. The young enthusiasts had little option but to accept the situation and put their campaign on hold.

For some women this was a traitorous abandonment of the cause and, as an alternative, their war-time campaigns included opposition to the 1914 Defence of the Realm Act, which would grant to the government wide-ranging emergency powers during the war. One element of that regulation states 'No person shall by word of mouth or in writing spread reports likely to cause disaffection or alarm among any of His Majesty's forces or among the civilian population' which meant that speaking out about there not being women's suffrage could be interpreted as contravening the Act.

With the Women's Suffrage struggle being put on hold for the foreseeable future, many young women, deprived of their crusade, looked to support the war effort out of a sense of duty. Their expectation was also that it presented an opportunity to demonstrate, in practical ways, the truths that they had been promoting in their campaign; women could make a valuable contribution to the country if given the opportunity. The supporters of women's suffrage included not militants alone, but also those supporting intellectual and philosophical viewpoints. Others were in neither of these two camps, but returned to their normal domestic lives, or went to work in factories, while the menfolk went overseas to fight.

The Women's Reserve Ambulance Corps (WRAC) satisfied Rotha Lintorn-Orman's needs in a number of ways, not the least being that it was a uniformed service comprising a khaki uniform with a badge depicting a green Maltese cross within a circle. Add to that a bronze title badge worn on the shoulder with the text 'Green Cross' and a pseudo military uniform is presented, all excepting the skirt which remains the last bastion of femininity.

The years at Forest Mere, embracing the masculine dress of the boy scouts, the paraphernalia of staff and knife and the discipline of drill and inspection, had been a heady concoction for a girl who had, to some extent, wanted to be rid of feminine restrictions. The origins of the Corps lay in the suffrage movement, in the person of Evelina Haverfield, whose first request to the Government had been to establish a Women's Volunteer Rifle Corps in order to support the Territorials in case of invasion.

The WRAC attracted young, upper middle class, women who could afford to take on unpaid voluntary work. Born out of desire rather than need, the work offered a level of adventure that they could not possibly have found in peacetime. The more extreme Suffragette activities had ceased with the outbreak of war, and the energies of those, who in the present day might be referred to as 'ladettes', sought other outlets.[3] The camaraderie of the Corps, the threat of danger and the public show of strength and control, was reward enough. Rotha had moved back to London, just off Baker Street in Cornwall Terrace Mews, and was caught up in the excitement of the capital city.

The role of Blanch Lintorn-Orman in her daughter's life is an interesting one. Whilst the family were in Forest Mere, during the scouting years, she took on the authoritative task of organising, both at Troop level and also at District level, the Scouts and later the Guides. It was Rotha, and Nesta, that had the inspiration and enthusiasm, but Blanch that took charge, even usurping what little power they had accumulated. Evelina Haverfield was Blanch's friend, or at least acquaintance, and it was she that directed Rotha towards the WRAC in response to their loyalist rallying call.

Evelina Haverfield's constant companion was born Vera Louise Holme in Lancashire; she and Haverfield lived together from 1911, and Vera became notorious for her cross dressing. She worked for some time on the stage as a 'male' impersonator, a pretence that spilled over into her life off stage. She spent some time as a suffragette and was described by Sylvia Pankhurst as 'a noisy, explosive young person, frequently rebuked by her elders for lack of dignity'. Having said that, she acquitted herself well in all the theatres of war in which she served.

In fact, Holme was less extreme than Haverfield in her support of the suffragettes. Holme spent time in prison for minor offences, but Haverfield was gaoled for more serious offences, including breaking into the House of Lords, criminal damage and attempting to disrupt a police cordon by leading police horses out of their ranks. In addition to Holme she set up the Foosack League, a secret organisation restricted to suffragettes who were also lesbians.

The WRAC had its headquarters at 199 Piccadilly and, in 1915, had a new Colonel in Command appointed in the person of Blanch Lintorn-Orman who presided over the 400 women that made up the WRAC, all in uniform. They were kitted out in khaki with a green cross armlet. It was this severe non-feminine attire that added to the attraction for young women of a certain persuasion; a persuasion to which Rotha seemed happy to succumb. Not only Rotha, but Blanch as well, who seemed to be happy to pose, at first in Girl Guide uniform and now in the uniform of the WRAC.

Blanch's appointment was a little strange, there being no sign of her having any interest in public service before this time. Rotha was now nineteen years old and barely out of her 'finishing' year in preparation for the adult life to come. The officers of the WRAC were obviously drawn from a small social group, of which Blanch was a member. It would not be unreasonable to make the assumption that Rotha's membership was a direct result of her mother's influence. The timing of

Blanch's appointment coincided with Evelina Haverfield's preparations to take up her role in Serbia.

Given that Blanch was integrated so readily into the WRAC, and at such a senior level, rather implies that her standing within the social group gathered around Evelina Haverfield was fairly high which, in turn, implies an acceptance of the Women's Suffrage cause. Where Blanch leads, then Rotha follows, so by further implication she was also a supporter, if not an activist, for that movement.

Rotha was listed as the WRAC's Motor Transport Officer, enabling her to satisfy a desire which had been denied her on the Oberammergau trip. She had both drivers and engineers under her command, although the drivers tended to look after their own vehicles as part of their job, and she had the ear of both the Colonel in Command and the overall power wielder, Evelina Haverfield, who was yet to begin her overseas war work. Blanch had again managed to out-rank her daughter, not only in Rotha's own chosen profession, but also in her circle of useful friends. It was tantamount to showing that Rotha needed Blanch to be able to achieve in life; that Rotha was nothing without Blanch.

Although the primary task of the WRAC was to assist servicemen arriving in London from the Front, injured and needing help to make their way home, the threat of danger was still very real. The operational base for the Corps was London Victoria Station, where trains to and from the Channel Ports departed and arrived, with members of the WRAC offering general assistance to those in need, whether civilian or military. Despite the criticisms that these young women were using the war as an opportunity to 'have the time of their lives', their dedication seems to have known no bounds.

The general atmosphere within the WRAC reflected that of Evelina Haverfield's own lifestyle, one of flying in the face of conformity. Married twice, with two sons, her second marriage was thought to be platonic in nature. Her lesbian affair was unusual, with Evelina keeping her own home but living with her friend Vera 'Jack' Holme.

She too was a controversial figure, who had previously worked with Emmeline, Sylvia and Christabel Pankhurst as their chauffeur. A pattern of young women, kicking over the traces of Victorian respectability, and defining their own lifestyle, was becoming more prevalent after 1914. In the midst of this transformation was Blanch Lintorn-Orman, either following Rotha's lead, or leading the way for Rotha to follow.

Press reports of the WRAC were not always critical. The *Illustrated War News*' assessment was that 'of all the societies and organisations . . . that the present conflict has called into being, none is doing better or more useful work than the Women's Reserve Ambulance', although others accused it of 'encroaching too closely on male territory'.

Funding for the WRAC was a matter of continuous concern, and advertisements were placed in the London newspapers asking for help. One such advertisement appeared in the *London Evening Standard*. As well as identifying its patrons, it mentioned specifically Colonel Mrs Lintorn-Orman and Captain Miss R. L. Lintorn-Orman as two of the officers. The WRAC described itself as providing orderlies in war hospital supply depots for the Royal Army Medical Corps and as supplying transport for military hospitals, some overseas. It's interesting that both Rotha and Blanch seemed at ease working within a formal military structure, both in uniform and both with a clearly defined rank.

As well as seeking funds, the WRAC was also in need of a London headquarters at a nominal rent; hitherto they had been working out of Blanch's home. Rotha, being in charge of transport, called specifically for the funding of garage and repair work, specifically for tyres, petrol, oil etc., but also looked for female volunteers who were able to contribute as motor mechanics. The WRAC did not have to rely entirely on its own advertising to promote its useful role.

> These ladies have organised themselves on military lines . . . undertake any kind of work . . . which Tommy declares he didn't join the army to do . . . scrubbing down, cleaning out, and otherwise preparing the Bethnal Green Hospital for its soldier occupants . . . cook, scrub, fetch and carry . . . Scores of men have been set free to enlist by the WRA[C] workers.[4]

Danger really presented itself on the evening of 8 September 1915 when German army zeppelins dropped bombs in the vicinity of Smithfield Market, St Paul's Cathedral and Liverpool Street Station, the first major raid of the conflict. The WRAC were immediately mobilised, were first on the scene, and helped tend the injured. The raid on London, dropping fifteen high explosive bombs and fifty-five incendiaries, caused over half a million pounds worth of damage. The young women, who had been having 'the time of their lives', showed their true mettle in that time of need, and the WRAC went on to support the authorities in numerous similar events to come.

The training that Rotha had received in the Girl Guides came into play, and the feelings of usefulness that she had experienced, following the Lake District collision between the ladies' coach and the hay cart, were not to be expected again while remaining at home. The WRAC was sending some units to France but for real adventure, in another all-women environment, it would take a different line of approach, one that was being taken even then by Evelina Haverfield.

Correspondents writing in various newspapers remarked on how poor the London defences were in countering the zeppelin attacks. Searchlights picked out the zeppelins in the dark but almost all the shells were very wide of their target, some were closer but only one possible hit was claimed. On one raid five aeroplanes took to the skies but only one managed to locate the zeppelin; it subsequently escaped in the fog. The Admiralty, which accepted responsibility for defence, undertook to improve matters.

The Admiralty appointed Sir Percy Morton Scott to take charge of defending Britain against zeppelin attack. His first step was to establish a London Air Defence Area equipped with high explosive shells able to ignite at the height of the target. He also recruited a small group of pilots capable of night flying and intercepting the zeppelins before they reached populated cities. By largely unofficial means, Scott managed to increase the number of London based anti-aircraft guns from 12 to 152 by the end of November of that year.

> He [Balfour] was asked why Sir Percy Scott had not been appointed before. The answer was that were things foreseen before the war and things not foreseen, and which could not have been foreseen, and one was the development of this method of warfare. It was now absolutely necessary to bring the whole Air Service more into harmony with the general practice of the Admiralty and greatly increase the staff . . . Although he could not promise immunity from aerial attack on London, he could promise that everything was being done to develop and organise such defences as were possible.[5]

Scott had retired in 1913 but was recalled at the outbreak of war with specific responsibility for the design and deployment of artillery. In the face of the zeppelin problem Scott took his plans to France where he directly commissioned a car manufacturer to start production quickly and efficiently. It was not that the British could not engineer the solution, but that the Admiralty red tape was too much of a hurdle to overcome in time.

Further raids took place on 13 October attacking various London targets, such as the Lyceum Theatre in the West End and Holborn, Charing Cross and Aldgate, but with improved London defences there were fewer bombing missions over the capital with the German offensive action having to be spread more widely across the country. The brief respite that rural areas had experienced since January, when airships had bombed the eastern counties, was to end with the war being brought to the doorstep of a much wider section of the population.

As the WRAC continued to demonstrate its value to the war effort, so it attracted the accolade of acquiring a popular appellation. The donations from the public grew as the WRAC gradually became known as *The Green Cross Corps*, from the insignia that they wore on their khaki uniform. The WRAC had plenty of young ladies to call upon who had learnt to drive on private estates and, for Rotha Beryl Lintorn-Orman, the opportunity for vehicle driving to be her personal contribution to Britain's fight against the Germans was of great satisfaction to her.

The influence of Evelina Haverfield upon Rotha was significant. Here was a woman who showed little regard for what was thought of as 'proper' behaviour, frowned upon the convention of heterosexual, even monogamous, relations and still sought adventure after the abandoned suffrage struggle. Haverfield decided to leave the WRAC and join a new group, again a product of the suffrage movement, that could offer her the challenge of overseas front-line action. Service overseas could also provide a more matriarchal environment than could be found in Britain; an all-women's group which could largely follow its own rules.

Rotha's maverick nature craved more action than could be found in London, and there was a real prospect that this other organisation might offer her a more satisfactory solution to her own frustrations. Evelina Haverfield, who was planning to take Vera Holme with her, was in a perfect position to clear the path for Rotha to join that new group. The opportunity to see action was exactly what Rotha was looking for and that, coupled with the prospect of working with motor vehicles that were soon to be employed in those conflict zones, was too much to turn down.

Given Blanch Lintorn-Orman's friendship with Evelina Haverfield, it is quite unthinkable that Rotha's mother would have had any objections to Rotha's voluntary enlistment. Rotha's father does not appear to have had any input either to the WRAC or to Rotha's or Blanch's lives; at this time there appears to be very few references to Charles and Blanch as a couple, although there are occasional mentions of them together in Bournemouth at Scout and Guide events. There is little evidence, one way or another, about how Blanch might have felt about Rotha's planned move away from her direct field of influence; although Blanch's contacts could have it stopped, had she so wished.

Blanch was living in both London and Somerset during this time. She was also involved with her war work in the city, and with the Girl Guide movement in the Bournemouth district where she still had responsibilities. Charles Lintorn-Orman is found in the Hampshire records, pursuing his own interests of composing and performing music, and being involved in local societies and events, where he is often listed in the newspapers as attending or making public addresses. There is no indication of Charles being involved in active military service.

Blanch, in addition to her continued association with Bournemouth through the Girl Guides, also formed a branch of the WRAC in the town.

> The Bournemouth branch of the Women's Reserve Ambulance was formed in June 1915. Its object was to provide a trained, disciplined and efficient body of

> women to help at war hospitals, and with other forms of emergency war work. The Battalion consisted of 45 members with 3 officers, all volunteers, who wore khaki uniform. In March 1916 the Battalion was presented with a Sunbeam Motor Ambulance which could take 4 stretchers, or 8 sitting cases. They assisted in moving wounded soldiers from the ambulance trains which arrived at Boscombe, Bournemouth Central and West, Christchurch and Wimborne Stations to the various hospitals in the district. All members were trained in the use of stretchers. The ambulance was also used to take soldiers to various entertainments and to take the Mont Dore [Military Hospital] nurses to and from their homes.[6]

There is evidence that early signs of the break-up of the marriage between Charles and Blanch pre-dated the onset of war by some years. Sir Lintorn's last will and testament not only leaves his entire estate to Blanch but also contains certain conditions and provisos designed to preclude Charles having any claim on the assets should the two separate. The will is dated 1901 and seems to indicate that Sir Lintorn was not convinced of Charles' suitability as a son-in-law, almost anticipating problems in the years to come.

*Chapter 6*

# Scottish Women's Hospital

Rotha's enlistment was into a non-combat organisation, not part of the Red Cross, but working alongside that organisation in bringing humanitarian relief to those suffering as a result of the conflict. The Scottish Women's Hospitals for Foreign Services (SWH) provided a destination for medical women, doctors and nurses, who were unable or unwilling to enlist into the Royal Army Medical Corps. In addition to qualified medical staff, the SWH also needed non-medical support staff, including ambulance drivers, and this was the goal to which Rotha's prayers had been directed.

The SWH, as previously mentioned, had its origins in the suffragist movement, in particular through the campaigning of Scottish born Elsie Maud Inglis, an Edinburgh surgeon. She, like many who had passed through the ranks of the suffrage movement, was also in a lesbian relationship. Elsie's partner was Flora Murray, who had worked as an anaesthetist at the Chelsea Hospital for Women and later founded the Women's Hospital for Children, in Harrow Road; at the outbreak of war Flora worked in Paris, as *Médecin-en-Chef* at a newly built hospital.

Inglis had been born in India, daughter and granddaughter of local magistrates, and relocated to Edinburgh when her father retired. She completed her education in Edinburgh and then at a Paris finishing school. She attended various medical schools, finally qualifying as a surgeon and then specialising in gynaecology and maternity. She was particularly concerned about her poorer patients and was known to waive her fees for needy cases. It was her concern about the status of women in society that led her to speak on behalf of the suffrage movement and supported many of the campaigns that they mounted.

At the outbreak of war Elsie Ingles' offers of help had been rejected by both the War Office and by the British Red Cross, the latter being under the effective control of the British Government; rather famously her offers of assistance were greeted with the response 'My good lady, go home and sit still'. Considering her suffragist background, this was a response calculated to engender a feeling of anger on the part of Elsie and her supporters, who did just the opposite of the advice that they received.

Anxious to prove the worth and capability of women, Inglis began campaigning for a hospital, staffed and managed solely by women, in order to aid the British war effort. A federation of all the non-militant women's suffragist societies got behind her with the intention of providing a fully equipped mobile hospital for the Allies in general, rather than just for British forces. Early reports were very clear that the initiative was on behalf of the suffragist movement, and so attracted recruits from supporters of that movement.

Associating the SWH with the suffrage movement, and making it very clear that Elsie Inglis was a prime mover, had the effect of encouraging more young women who were looking for an outlet for their energies, and young women who shared a more masculine outlook on life. Certainly, those women who joined the SWH were to follow the axiom of 'to work hard, and to play hard'; their hard work was applauded, their hard play was often criticised as being unladylike.

The first announcement about the hospital appeared in the September edition of the journal of the National Union of Women's Suffrage Societies (NUWSS), claiming that several women doctors, nurses and dressers had already offered their services and that a further £100 were needed to complete the task. In fact, as was confirmed in a letter from Inglis, published in the next edition of the journal, the amount required was nearer to £1,000.

> The Scottish Federation appeals for £100 to enable it to start fair upon a scheme which it has in view. This scheme, proposed by Dr Elsie Inglis, Secretary of the Federation, is to provide a mobile Red Cross Hospital for work at the front, either in connection with British, French, or Belgian troops, as may be most suitable. Already donations of £12 have been received. Several women doctors, nurses and dressers have volunteered their services, and one lady has offered to go as interpreter. All that is now wanted is monetary assistance.[1]

In reality, a figure nearer to £5,000 was required, but it was hoped that some of the senior medical staff would waive their stipends; junior staff and ancillaries were expected to serve as unpaid volunteers. There was some initial disagreement over the name, specifically the use of the word 'Scottish' rather than 'British' and the absence of 'suffrage' from the name. The matter was finally resolved and the name 'Scottish Women's Hospitals for Foreign Services' was finally agreed upon and adopted, although they were generally known simply as the 'Scottish Women's Hospitals'.

The initiative was not entirely without criticism. A letter published in the *St. Andrews Citizen* under the headline Political Patriotism, claimed that it was merely a base attempt 'to exploit the war and the sufferings of our gallant troops to further the ends of a particular section' by which they meant political controversy in favour of women's suffrage. Readers were quick to rebut the criticisms, claiming that the SWH were proud of their politics and had garnered support and funds from many who did not share their suffragist opinions. There were other letters published that sought to discourage giving any assistance to privately sponsored hospitals.

The results of this initial appeal were disappointing, with a meagre £213 raised by the middle of October, but the situation was greatly improved once fund raising and recruitment activities were extended beyond Scotland and into other parts of the country. Despite the fact that the mobile hospitals were to operate under the umbrella name of Scottish Women's Hospitals for Foreign Services, much of the funding actually originated via the new London office.[2]

Recruitment was also strong over the entire south of England with many of the women offering their services prompted, not just by their desire to demonstrate the power of women as a means to advance the cause of women's suffrage, but by the common bond of having their menfolk serving overseas, and by their humanity in the treatment of the victims of war. It seems that for many of the young non-medical recruits this was a 'call to arms', satisfying their need for adventure, not dissimilar to that of their male counterparts who volunteered to fight rather than waiting to be conscripted.

Commenting on the difficulties of persuading the male dominated military establishment, Inglis reminded her followers of the suffragist origins of the struggle: 'The ordinary male disbelief in our capacity cannot be argued away. It can only be worked away'.[3] The SWH, having been rejected by the 'establishment', was firmly rooted in the women's movement that had postponed its militant struggle at the outbreak of war, but was not insensitive to the deeper feelings of its most ardent volunteers.

Although the foundations of the SWH clearly lay in the suffragist movement, as time went by more and more funding and recruitment was from outside that movement. Consequently the NUWSS was forced to loosen its grip on SWH and control gradually developed into the less militant Hospitals Committee, which then began to take the reins and manage under a less idealistic ethos. This, of course, meant that voices within the organisation could be more critical of the behaviour and ethics of the 'rank and file'.

The first mobile hospital to be established was in Calais, with many Belgian soldiers being treated by Dr Antoine Depage, who had relocated from Brussels at the outbreak of war in order to develop a large Red Cross hospital under the auspices of the Belgian Queen Elizabeth, who in turn had been encouraged to leave the capital through fears of her possible capture by German forces. Depage had left behind him *l'École Belge d'Infirmières Diplômées* in the Rue de la Culture, the nursing school to which Edith Cavell was appointed as director, and from where she operated the Allied escape route through the Netherlands and then back to Britain where men were, after a short rest, redeployed back to the front line.[4]

The initial experience in Calais was one of resentment on the part of the French and Belgian army generals who were not enthusiastic about the SWH presence. Depage had requested a few nurses to assist in the hospital, but was pressured into handing over a fifty bed annex to form a viable unit for a much larger contingent from the SWH, to deal with a typhoid epidemic. As the number of patients grew so did the problem of clearing beds as there were no plans for convalescence in place, but by the middle November the epidemic could be said to be over, and the SWH unit was stood down.

A second SWH mobile hospital was established just to the north of Paris at Royaumont Abbey working with the French Red Cross and designated as *Hôpital Auxiliaire* 301. It was never affiliated with either the British military or Red Cross and almost exclusively treated the French or French colonials who were injured. *Hôpital Auxiliaire 301* was the largest British voluntary hospital in France and developed a satellite operation at Villers-Cotterêts, even closer to the front line. One of those working for the SWH at *Hôpital Auxiliaire 301* was the artist Norah Neilson Gray, who produced two of her best known works featuring contemporary scenes from that hospital.

The SWH hospitals in France were largely staffed by women who had originally been specifically recruited for service in Serbia, but had then been redirected to support the troops in the trenches when the enormity of the casualty toll in France became clear. This was a static war and the concept of a mobile hospital unit was more attuned to a conflict of skirmish and moving battles, rather than to one of static attrition. The surge of recruitment, and of financial contributions, had been driven more by the thought of tending to the random sufferings of troops and civilians in Serbia than for being a cog in the machinery of a sedentary stand-off on the Western Front.

The SWH sent its first contingent bound for Serbia very early in 1915 under Elsie Inglis, who initially set up three mobile hospitals at Kragujevac, Mladenovac and Valjevo. The second contingent had left England in April 1915, with a planned stopover at Malta after the first five days of sailing. However, with wounded soldiers expected to arrive from the Dardanelles, this second mobile hospital was commandeered by the local medical authorities and asked to assist in Malta; so this second contingent destined for Serbia did not actually arrive at their destination until early June, with Evelina Haverfield as the administrator.

The appointment of Evelina Haverfield, whose function was that of 'administrator' was unusual in that she volunteered her services to SWH but was never formally appointed to that position; rather she took on the role on a trial basis. It was stipulated that she must promise to obey orders, and that SWH was not committed to keeping her on should she not prove useful. There was an obvious fear that her time with the Pankhursts and Women's Social and Political Union, which had led to two periods in prison, might cause problems in Serbia.

While the second contingent was still establishing itself in Serbia, events overtook the entire SWH presence in that country. Bulgaria, that had yet to issue a formal declaration of war, began to attack Serbia, advancing to link up with the German Eleventh Army; at the same time Bulgarian forces began to push into Macedonia, thereby cutting off the Serbian army from Allied support and reinforcements. Although both French and British troops attempted to break the blockade, somewhat obstructed by Greece, they were reluctant to push too far into enemy controlled territory.

Belgrade fell to the enemy in October 1915, followed by Mladenovac and Valjevo. The SWH mobile hospitals re-formed at Kragujevac but most of the staff had finally to retreat over the mountains to Albania, although some decided to stay with their patients. The Germans were courteous to the medical staff, but ruthless in their persecution of the Serbs, and took over the Kragujevac hospital for their own wounded, the SWH staff being transferred to the Czar Lazar military hospital along with all their Serbian patients. Diphtheria and typhus were raging among the Serbian troops, and at the Czar Lazar the SWH found the hospital to be in a poor condition without sanitation and with the only water supply being from a broken pump, more than 100 metres away across open ground.[5]

In these dire circumstances, Evelina Haverfield more than fulfilled that which was required of her as an administrator. She and Vera Holme, who accompanied her, acted much as nursing staff, tending to patients, fetching and carrying, visiting injured civilians in the town. There was a great deal of looting and 'even the Serbian Red Cross magazine was being robbed of its stores. Mrs Haverfield herself was one morning sitting at the door of these stores with a loaded revolver, as it was the only way to keep the thieves away'.[6]

Eventually most SWH staff had to be repatriated to Thessaloniki (Salonica) in Greece, including a contingent that had been financed from Cambridge and carried the appellation of Girton and Newnham, both women's colleges at that university, and both with very vocal suffrage societies. The staff that remained in Serbia were classified as prisoners of war and received much the same treatment as other prisoners who had been combatants. These last few members of SWH were finally released and transported home via Switzerland, reaching London in February 1916.

All this had taken place while Rotha Lintorn-Orman was volunteering with WRAC in London and she would have undoubtedly been aware that the founder of that organisation, Evelina Haverfield, had been in Serbia with the SWH and was now back in London, and approachable. Rotha's strong desire for a front line driving role would be more than satisfied should she be allowed to serve in a conflict zone, and where better than from where Evelina Haverfield had recently returned. With her mother's connection to Haverfield, and her own previous service with her in the WRAC, her wish was easily granted.

Three months later, in May 1916, with the new Allied offensive planned, a SWH unit was being prepared to be sent to Macedonia, for which funds were secured from America and Canada; honorary secretary Kathleen Burke, of the London office, had been on a one-woman fund raising campaign in

North America. In return for the £10,000 donated, the new hospital unit was to be called the American Unit and was to comprise not only medical staff, but also a sixty strong transport column.

This was the trigger that catapulted Rotha Lintorn-Orman into her overseas war service. At last she was going to be able to put the skills and attitudes that she had developed and honed during her scouting and guiding years at Forest Mere, to the test. Out in the wilds of Serbia, the years of camping, bivouacking, cooking and self-sufficiency would show their worth. In August of 1916 Rotha joined the Scottish Women's Hospitals for Foreign Service and prepared for adventure.

> Miss Lintorn-Orman, who is on her way to Serbia as an ambulance driver for the Scottish Women's Hospital Unit which is to be attached to the Serbian Army, is the granddaughter of the late Field-Marshal Sir Lintorn Simmons. She has been at work since the war began on behalf of the wounded. An excellent driver and a good worker, her training for a time was under the wing of the Women's Reserve Ambulance. She now joins the Serbian Army in the Near East.[7]

Nesta Maude, Rotha's companion at Forest Mere, after a period working on the land also found work driving. She joined the Royal Flying Corps, driving all types of vehicle including cars, lorries and large transport vehicles and trailers. She writes, in her autobiography, that she frequently drove the 'crash tender' that attended crashed aeroplanes, along with ambulances and fire tenders, which meant long periods of duty, and not being stood down until all aircraft had been accounted for.

Oswald Mosley, during this time, had already served in France on the Western Front before transferring to the Royal Flying Corps where he served as both a pilot and an observer. His recklessness led to him crash his aeroplane whilst 'showing off', resulting in him being moved back to the trenches, only to be invalided back home to a desk job in Whitehall.

*Chapter 7*

# The American Unit

It was to the American Unit, financed by Kathleen Burke's spring time visit to the United States of America, that Rotha Lintorn-Orman was assigned in August 1916, as a volunteer driver with the SWH during its planned assignment overseas. Much of the information about the American Unit, also known as the Ostrovo Unit, comes from Leah Leneman's book *In the Service of Life*, the biography of Elsie Inglis.

This all-female unit, again, had its origins in the suffragist movement with an easy acceptance of same sex relationships, such as that between Dr Lilian Cooper and her companion Josephine Bedford who 'had worshipped each other from the early days of their youth'. Cooper and Bedford had both returned from Australia to contribute to the British war effort. Bedford, not medically trained, travelled with the American Unit only because Dr Cooper was unable to function properly without her. Lacking a formal role Bedford unofficially took charge of the motor department: vehicles, chauffeurs, tools and accessories.

Dr Lilian Victoria Cooper arrived in Brisbane in 1891, four years before Rotha was born, with Mary Josephine Bedford, her long term partner. Cooper's route to the SWH broadly followed that of Elsie Inglis in that she originally volunteered her service, in her case to the Australian Army who did not 'need' female doctors, so sought work with an organisation that did. Josephine Bedford was her long term companion and driving force behind her 'partner', ferrying her around her practice and undertaking many good works on her own account.

Closer to the day-to-day operational life of Rotha Lintorn-Orman were Elsie Corbett and Kathleen Dillon, who had met on their first journey to Serbia, entered into a very personal relationship, and would eventually stay together until separated by death in the 1950s. Both Corbett and Dillon had been held as prisoners of war after Belgrade fell to the enemy, but had eventually been repatriated. They were both drivers, although they had originally been intended for assignment to Russia as nursing orderlies; they had both retrained as drivers in order to stay together and to sail with the American Unit to Serbia.

Elsie Cameron Corbett was the daughter of a baron, another example of recruitment from the aristocracy, and was also an avid supporter of the women's suffrage campaign and enjoyed behaving unconventionally. She was a major fund raiser for SWH and for the 'Scottish Lassie' motorised ambulances for the hospitals nearest the front. She trained as a nurse so that she could volunteer with the SWH and travel to Serbia, where she met Kathleen Nora Dillon, her future lifelong companion.

The sexual orientation of these women was irrelevant to their achievements, and although there is no direct evidence regarding Rotha Lintorn-Orman's own preferences at this time, such a liberal attitude must have made volunteering with SWH a more comfortable option for her than would have been the case with an orthodox mainstream organisation. It was well known that Evelina Haverfield was in a long term relationship with Vera Holme, and that both were there at their own expense. The couple 'appearing to have been as "married" as any heterosexual couple could be' were quite comfortable in that group, and individual members of that group must have been quite comfortable in their presence.

The war obviously threw young women together where they were free to experience and express a degree of camaraderie in their shared danger that had hitherto been the preserve of young male warriors. They were free of parental control and able to indulge themselves in blurring the traditional differences of dress and behaviour. Ten years after the war a novel, *The Well of Loneliness* by Radclyffe Hall, exposed the mannish dress and behaviour of female ambulance drivers serving in France; it seems probable that the same could be applied to Serbia.

In the novel, wartime hospital work provided a publicly acceptable role for lesbian women to perform. Their 'inversion',[1] once out in the open could not be hidden again from the mainstream view and they are likened to shell-shocked soldiers, psychologically damaged by their status as outcasts. The main character of the novel, expected to be born a boy by her parents, but is actually a girl, is nevertheless named Stephen and as she grows takes on masculine dress and mannerisms.

Rachel Michelle Brown in her published thesis[2] makes an interesting point by claiming that the middle and upper class young women drawn to the voluntary organisations such as SWH, were generally more socially confident than were their working class contemporaries, and were therefore less likely to exercise self-restraint in adopting mannish style dress and hairstyles. Their liberation in dress could quite easily develop into an increased sexual freedom, both heterosexual and homosexual, and that such example would encourage their working class contemporaries to adopt the same, fuelled by the added urgency of war.

The transport column of the American Unit set sail for Thessaloniki (Salonica) under the command of Mrs Kate Harley on 3 August 1916, but there was tension between medical and non-medical personnel from the outset. This seems to have stemmed from the 'no-smoking in public' rule that the drivers in particular objected to; these drivers were, right from the start, a disruptive force. Not in the least because they had not been subject to the same rigorous training routines of the nursing staff, nor been subject to the tight discipline regimes so prevalent in hospitals.

The non-medical women, orderlies as well as drivers, were described as undisciplined, walking around the deck smoking and making themselves generally conspicuous; behaviour that one might expect from young men rather than from young ladies. The authoritarian overlords of the SWH did not seem to recognise that these young women, away from their families and on their way into a conflict zone, were in every way performing as might be expected of young men going to war, and were likely to manifest their fears and apprehensions in a similar manner.

Ten days after sailing from Britain, the ship docked at Thessaloniki only to be informed that, instead of forming a base hospital at the port, the mobile hospital was to be established at Ostrovo, some eighty-five miles nearer the fighting in Macedonia. The transport column was, again, subject to more criticisms of undisciplined behaviour and of mannish mannerisms and dress. Most drivers had their hair cut short and many were considered as 'fairly butch'; one of the medical staff commented that they 'might be men' and another 'one wonders what sex they are'. The members of the transport column were considered as being 'very bold and bad'.[3]

Before the main body of women set out for Ostrovo, an advanced party led by Agnes Bennett preceded them north. What Bennett found there was 'a picturesque spot beside a large lake', the party being met by a group of Serbian officers, who were very attentive to the newcomers. Dr Bennett remarked upon the Serbian practice of gallantly kissing the hands of the ladies to whom they were introduced, but did not speculate on how such attentions might be received, and responded to, by the ambulance drivers of the American Unit.

While Dr Bennett was undertaking her visit to Ostrovo the American Unit set up a temporary base at Thessaloniki railway station with the transport column camped nearby. There were complaints that the conduct of the transport column was constantly unsettling the main body of nurses and that Mrs Harley's ideas of discipline were unsettling. There was some relief when the transport column finally departed for Ostrovo.

Although there is much evidence of a culture of lesbianism and 'laddish' behaviour within the SWH, and within the American Unit in particular, it was by no means universal. In the main the medical staff, both doctors and nurses, spurned that culture, as did many of the orderlies and general staff. It was the drivers, young women who had looked to replace the excitement of the campaign for women's suffrage, especially those that had experienced the suffragette initiative, or were frustrated at being denied the opportunity to rebel, who fell into that category.

It should be remembered that many of the nurses and orderlies were married or betrothed women, with their husbands or fiancés serving in one of the theatres of war, and so were not available for casual relationships. Even if they were so disposed the availability of men was limited to the injured and maimed, who would by their very nature be transient, there being very few men travelling with the mobile hospital. Anyway, such dalliances would have come to the notice of hospital discipline, and been dealt with firmly.

The journey to Ostrovo was gruelling, crossing vast plains and encountering all manner of obstacles from camels to motor cars, and from mules to motor lorries. On passing through the mountains, the roads were quite frightening with narrow paths and dangerous precipices. Arriving at Ostrovo, the main American Unit found matters far from satisfactory, most of the advance party having succumbed to malaria or dysentery. These outbreaks were not just confined to Ostrovo, but plagued that entire theatre of war.

Death from malaria came quickly to the American Unit in Ostrovo when Olive Smith, a masseuse and physical training instructor from Northumberland who worked in the operating theatre, died of cerebral malaria within two months of joining SWH and within a week or two of arriving in the war zone. Her death was keenly felt and her body was taken to Thessaloniki for burial. Approximate figures suggest that malaria claimed more than 400 Allied non-combatant lives during the war, with

*Right*: Field Marshal John Lintorn Arabin Simmons as portrayed in *Vanity Fair*.

*Below*: Deasy motorcar circa 1906.

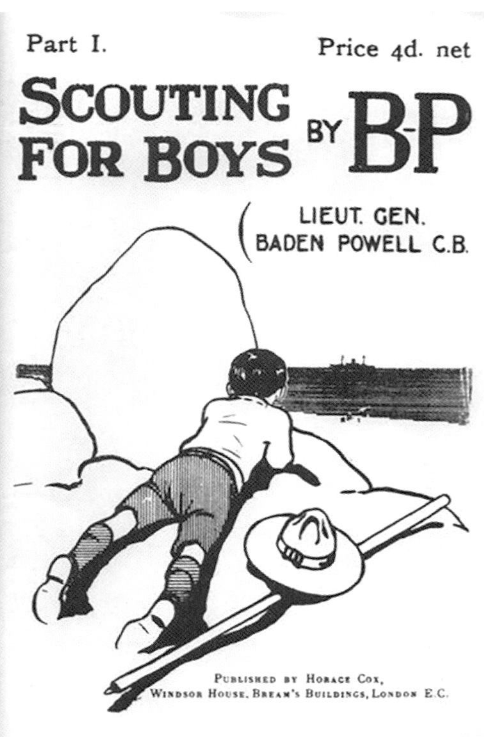


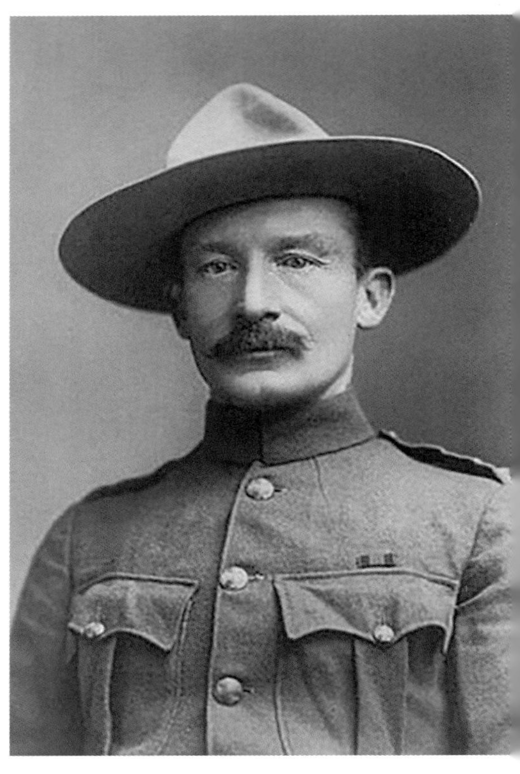

*Above left*: *Scouting for Boys.*

*Above right*: Lord Robert Baden-Powell.

*Left*: L-R: Rotha Orman, Blanch Orman and Nesta Maude.

*Above left*: National Scout Rally at the Crystal Palace.

*Above right*: Elsie Maud Inglis.

*Below*: SWH nurses in Serbia.

*Above*: Ostrovo, on the Gornichevo Ridge.

*Left*: Evelina Haverfield.

The Kibbo Kift Kindred.

*Above left*: Robert Byron Drury Blakeney.

*Above right*: Rotha Lintorn-Orman.

*Above left*: Sir Oswald Mosley.

*Above right*: Emmeline Pankhurst.

British Fascists lapel pin badge.

The General Strike.

Grave of Rotha Lintorn-Orman in Las Palmas Cemetery.

*Left*: Field Marshal John Lintorn Arabin Simmons.

*Below*: Vera Louise Holme.

many more amongst soldiers living in even more primitive and unsanitary conditions.

On 12 September 1916 fighting broke out just a few miles from Ostrovo, on the Gornichevo ridge and the SWH began taking in casualties. Over the following eight weeks casualties totalled 425, only ending with the Allies signing an armistice with Bulgarian forces. During that time the transport column ferried injured combatants directly from the battlefield to dressing stations, such journeys being undertaken in the most rigorous conditions; and then from the dressing stations to the field hospital. The transport column, while working courageously, continued to be a problem to manage, even to the extent of driving their vehicles onto the battleground when expressly forbidden to do so.

Accounts of the action at the Gornichevo ridge were shocking, being described as a truly racial fight between the Serbians and Bulgarians, inflicting terrible wounds upon each other. On that first day all the transport and drivers were at the front line to bring back a multitude of casualties, many of whom had suffered grotesque injuries to stomach and chest as well as a multitude of compound fractures, a good number of patients dying in transit. Even while Rotha and her fellow drivers were being praised for their outstanding service under fire, they were still proving difficult to work with, operating outside the norms of expected attitudes and behaviour, and showing a lack of respect for authority.

The drivers, while doing valuable work and achieving more than was expected of them, were undisciplined but this was attributed to the lack of control exercised by Kate Harley, partly due to her age, partly due to her pugnacious nature. The solution to the driver problem was to hand over their day-to-day management entirely to Josephine Bedford, which did seem to temper the problem a little. Bedford, being a little older than the majority of drivers, managed to mollify them and calm down a little of their rebelliousness. Perhaps simply confining the management of the drivers to someone not so confrontational as Kate Harley was the solution, to give that responsibility to someone who could take over control, establish some level of trust, and shield the drivers from some of the concentrated criticism that was coming from all sides.

Attempts to persuade Harley to resign fell on deaf ears, she knew little about the vehicles that were part of her unit, but also repudiated the opinions of those who did, thus exacerbating the situation. Agnes Bennett wrote that the 'wily old woman' refused to resign and that she was 'spoiling the game for us here'. Even the Serbs were surprised that she was still in post. In the end there seemed to be no alternative but to dismiss her, but before that happened Miss Agneta Beauchamp from the Headquarters Committee wrote a letter to Harley such that she could do little else but resign.

It was not only Kate Harley that was proving a difficulty. Evelina Haverfield had given some cause for concern over her inability to hide her dislike of some of the others with whom she had to work and co-operate. Others felt that her administrative skills were lacking, in both efficiency and organisation. In hindsight it seems probable that Haverfield had experienced some form of breakdown through her unrelenting hard work.

As a consequence a number of senior staff had resigned, either to go home or to join other units. On one of her trips back home to Britain, Evelina Haverfield found that London SWH was unwilling to return her to Serbia. Her war was over.

Thus, by the end of October the SWH headquarters had finally dealt with Kate Harley, who was generally agreed to have been impossible to work with, and who allowed her drivers to behave foolishly and without discipline. Her removal from post had been a difficult business to manage, but it had been accomplished without undue disturbance, particularly as Mrs Agnes Harley was the sister of Field Marshal Sir John French, the first commander of the British Expeditionary Force. The important distinction to make here is that Kate Harley did not encourage indiscipline, but through her lack of measured control, could not prevent it. In turn, she herself was also difficult to control, refusing deployment where and when instructed and even recklessly pitching camp much too near the front line.

Of the drivers, there was no criticism of the work they undertook, nor of their work ethic, and they certainly did not indulge in any of the usual girlish nonsense that might have been expected with so many men around. The flying transport column, now removed from Mrs Harley's control, was attached directly to the hospital management. This was as much to counter her historical indiscipline against higher command, as to attempt to change the behaviour of the drivers.

Under this new management the transport column was no less undisciplined. They were said to swear, to discard their skirts in favour of breeches and that there were suggestions of very unseemly behaviour amongst them. Although not specifically stated, this would seem to imply female to female behaviour, not entirely unexpected considering that the column was drawn from young middle and upper class members of the pre-war suffrage movement, where such relationships were not uncommon.

Agnes Bennett, who ran the hospital to which the drivers were now attached, wrote before their transfer directly to hospital management, of the difficulties in controlling the young women.

> One of the troubles here is, that the girls would, many of them, like to discard skirts altogether, and now they hear that Dr Inglis' Unit are going about in boy scouts' costumes they are getting restless again. I am very much afraid that the girls do tend to get rough – those especially that go much about the roads . . . the swear words I have heard the drivers of other units use, have made me curl up inside when I think of them coming from a girl's lips, I am told that much worse expressions are quite common. It does disgust me very much and one feels it is not good for the men to see it and hear it. If they must be like men, let them be gentlemen, one said to me, not like the roughest Tommy.[4]

The use of the words 'boy scouts' reflect Rotha's childhood interests, if not her obsessions, and her influence must surely have been brought to bear on her fellow drivers in adopting that form of dress. The masculine boy scouts dress had been widely adopted by girl scouts in the years around the Crystal Palace rally, but the long skirt had always taken preference over trousers or breeches. In Serbia, doing the work that they did and climbing in and out of large transport vehicles, the girl drivers had an opportunity to cite common sense and expediency in support of their preference of dress. It fell upon deaf ears.

There were other worries concerning the drivers, about their sexuality and the rumours that were circulating about relationships between the girls. Two of the drivers were dismissed and, on their return to Britain the Red Cross advised that they should no longer be considered for overseas work. '. . . sheds an interesting light on the boarding-school values of these young women, dismissed in such disgrace'.

Christmas 1916 was celebrated in a much calmer atmosphere than might have been the case had Mrs Harley still had command of the transport column, but after the new year the entire Ostrovo Unit rebelled against further changes to the local management structure. The suggestion had been mooted that Agnes Bennett should have her unit halved by handing over 100 beds, and associated staff, to Dr Alice Hutchinson at Vodena. The reaction of the non-medical staff, orderlies and drivers, was that they would not accept such a move and reminded the authorities that it was the non-medical staff that ruled any hospital, and they would not work under anyone but Bennett. This militant unit won the day and the proposed local changes of senior personnel were reversed.

*Chapter 8*

# Repatriation from Greece

During those turbulent times the plague of malaria continued to take its toll on the American Unit, and in January 1917, Rotha Lintorn-Orman contracted the disease. This meant her immediate evacuation back to Thessaloniki for hospitalisation, with the intention of returning her to Britain once she had recovered from the illness. Recovery was by no means certain, even less so in the cold Serbian winter, lying in a hospital tent, with a patient to nurse ratio that would have been intolerable back in Britain.

Malaria was a very nasty disease, with unpleasant symptoms and side effects. For a young woman of twenty-two the symptoms would most likely present themselves as intense periods of fever, with heavy sweating, shivering, headache, and muscle pain. Add to these the symptoms of dysentery and it becomes a ghastly experience for both patient and nurse. Even after the worst period of the disease had passed, repeated bouts could still plague the sufferer, sometimes occurring so closely one after the other that the illness appears to be continuous.

> Dr McIlroy describes treating malaria, jaundice, pneumonia, typhoid, paratyphoid, influenza, dengue and sandfly fever. She outlines some of the treatment regimens employed. Patients with malaria were often

> delirious and required constant nursing attention and it was difficult to keep them cool as both ice and fans were in short supply. Intra-muscular injections of quinine were given every six hours until their temperature fell.[1]

The overland journey from Ostrovo to Thessaloniki must have been unbearable for Rotha, and other patients that had fallen foul of the disease. Patients could not stay in the field hospital until they were fully cured and fit to travel, as beds and nursing care were needed for much more urgent cases. So the journey was undertaken at the earliest possible moment in their recovery. Taking into consideration that Rotha's general health suffered in the following years it is very possible that the infections, and a lack of proper convalescence, counted towards her later difficulties.

Even if Rotha did not suffer cerebral malaria, as did Olive Smith, then long term neurological complications could still occur. The malaria parasite can remain in the body for many years, not necessarily inducing fevers during that time, thus remaining untreated. Complications in later life could occur following acute organ failure and other metabolic dysfunctions that might present themselves as a consequence of excessive alcohol or drug abuse. This could explain the severe health problems that Rotha experienced as a consequence of her indulgent later lifestyle.

It was during Rotha's period of illness, and the start of her repatriation back to Britain, that a singular event occurred which would colour her post war life and attitudes. At the beginning of February 1917, workers in Russia, specifically in

Petrograd, began a series of strikes and demonstrations against Tsar Nicholas II and his government. The demonstrations and strikes spread and by 11 March the situation was concerning enough for the Tsar to instruct the army to intervene using force; the result was mutiny. Six days later the Royal Family were placed under house arrest, and the arrival of Vladimir Lenin from Switzerland, and the increasing popularity of the Bolsheviks heralded the final overthrow of the established order.

The initial reaction in Whitehall was one of support for the Tsar's overthrow, none more enthusiastic than the Prime Minister, David Lloyd George who regarded it as 'the first great triumph of the principle for which we entered the war... the cause of human freedom'. However, inside Russia, conditions were worsening under the Provisional Government and the Bolsheviks were reaping the benefits of the growing discontent. As the Bolshevik influence increased, so did the British fear of the consequences.

The greatest fear in Britain was that an inward looking Russia, under a new government, might turn its back on the allied cause and make a separate peace with Germany leaving the entire eastern front exposed. The British Government feared that it would come under severe criticism if valuable resource were spent in bolstering this new regime. Not all of Russia supported the revolutionary government and the British were divided on how to support only one faction amongst many.

The Labour party considered that the events in Russia were clearing away 'the paraphernalia of medieval feudalism', while others feared the growing support for the Bolshevik movement within the working classes and they feared for a future which was dominated by International Socialism, putting at risk Britain's overseas investments. Even those industrial investments inside Great Britain were at risk from trades unions seizing control of the means of production. Such concerns were most keenly felt within the Conservative Party and its wider supporters.

The changing situation in Russia led to difficulties for the western allies and, in particular, for the members of the SWH in Russia, many of whom were coming to the end of their tour of duty. Their return home was not hampered by the new regime, but the British government was reluctant to sanction others being sent to Russia to replace them. As well as malaria, those left behind were subject to suspicion and interrogation, as were many other western Europeans; spy fever was also raging.

Rotha Lintorn-Orman, convalescing in Thessaloniki, had come from a wealthy military family, her grandfather embodying the very essence of being a monarchist. Every part of her history and background caused her to resent the overthrow of the Tsar, and the imprisoning of the establishment figures who supported the Royal Family. The enemy was clearly socialism, communism not yet having become established as an overriding term for the extreme left wing of politics. The most outspoken opponent of the extreme left wing was to be found in Italy:one time socialist, now a disillusioned poacher turned gamekeeper, Benito Mussolini.

At the start of the war, Mussolini had been a member of the Italian Socialist Party, but was forced out of the party because of his support for intervention in the conflict. He favoured a form of national socialism that turned its back on the conventional class struggle in order to advocate a more progressive approach that called upon a pro-active, pro-national movement, irrespective of class. His view was that elected representatives were not necessarily the best to make decisions, and that there was a role for experts, those who 'knew best'. This could be said to be the early annunciation of what was to become Mussolini's vision of fascism.

When Mussolini was invalided out of the army, with an exemplary service record, he turned back to writing, this time for the *Il Popolo d'Italia*, where he further developed and proclaimed his theories. His views were not entirely at odds with the British Government, even receiving a stipend from Sir Samuel Hoare of MI5 to print pro-war propaganda material in his newspaper.[2] With this tacit British approval, his anti-socialist views found support among the British patriotic right wing, none less than from that section of the community which included the Lintorn-Orman family.

Martin Pugh, in his book *Hurrah for the Blackshirts*, argues that the war brought about a political climate that could accommodate a fascist dimension in putting country before party and before self. There was a patriotic belief in an overriding need and right of the country to an individual's loyalty, and at the same time distrusting all foreigners and foreign institutions. There was a general fear of spies and fifth columnists, a fear which the Government fostered, causing the country to look in on itself and turn against internationalism. Could this groundswell of patriotism be harnessed when the war was over, and developed into a movement that would make Britain and the Empire prosper?

Rotha had time to consider such things as she recovered her health in Thessaloniki, waiting for passage home. The city was known as the Jerusalem of the Balkans, a melting pot of nationalities and peoples, more than 60,000 of whom were Jews, and was the centre of operations for allied forces in the Balkans. As well as the Jews, there were 40,000 Orthodox Greeks and 45,000 Turks and another 10,000 people made up of various nationalities. The high population density and the absence of any social housing dramatically exacerbated the poor sanitary conditions in the city and meant that the western European population founded their own districts outside the central area.

In August 1917 the city of Thessaloniki suffered a tragedy of monumental proportions, not as a direct result of, but as an indirect consequence of, the conflict. A small house in the Mevlane district accidentally caught fire and, because of a strong wind, known locally as *Vardaris*, quickly spread to adjoining properties, and eventually to the entire central part of the city. The fire burned for thirty-two hours, eventually dying out rather than being extinguished, the city having lost approximately 9,500 houses.

The city had no dedicated fire brigade but relied upon small, independent insurance companies' fire-fighting teams who were inefficient and primarily interested only in protecting the property of their own subscribers. The situation was exacerbated by the fact that the water supply was under the control of the Allies who were concerned with conserving water for their own army camps and hospitals in the suburbs. Added to this, the city was suffering from a summer drought and there were more and more refugees arriving to increase demand on a limited water supply.

Accounts of the fire speak of an avenue of flames, a mile wide, that destroyed everything in its path. A letter home from Second Lieutenant John Ewart Shillito provides a first-hand account of the fire, including the role played by SWH and other medical groups.

> . . . stream of refugees and homeless children steadily grew and by 8.30pm all the front was just one surging mass of moving furniture of every description and men, women, boys & girls & children in arms, literally thousands . . . All the notable churches were ablaze and French engineers were already beginning to dynamite large sections of buildings around the fire in an endeavour to localise it . . . British ambulances were evacuating the sick and aged Turks, Jews and Greeks and the rest, many of whom absolutely refused to budge from their doorsteps until the flames actually drove them out . . . huge chunks of fire were being blown along with the wind and out at sea one or two ships had already caught alight . . . The fire had spread like lightning on the wind and not only the front but all the fishing boats moored up to the water's edge were blazing away, many of them filled with the poor refugees.[3]

During the conflagration the SWH transport column, those that were in Thessaloniki for whatever reason, transported thousands of people to safety while the fire burned, putting themselves and their vehicles at risk. In the aftermath British and French troops assisted many victims, both countries setting up tented camps to house those left homeless and to transport some to other cities. The Red Cross and the SWH played a prominent part in the relief work, with members of the transport column carrying families from the city to the new tented camps or to the railway station for onward travel to Athens, Volos, Larissa and other Greek cities.

Rotha, now reasonably recovered from malaria was able to assist in the evacuation from both the fire and from the aftermath. The SWH camp was on the outskirts of the city so was not itself in danger from the fire, but personnel, both drivers and medical staff, provided what help they could. The drivers being, particularly courageous while the fire was at its height, were later decorated by the Greek government for their contribution. Thus, Rotha was to add to the two Serbian Croix de Charité medals, sometimes known as the Samaritans Cross, which she was awarded for her war efforts in Serbia.

> British ambulances were evacuating the sick and aged Turks, Jews and Greeks and the rest, many of whom absolutely refused to budge from their doorsteps until the flames actually drove them out . . . In the street were long convoys of transports going in every direction and on the sea side of the street were the helpless refugees three and four deep for a mile seated on their belongings, hysterical girls shrieking in the weirdest manner all the time.[4]

Rotha was eventually repatriated, but once back in Britain, with the country still at war, she was in search of a suitable role to fill. What she could offer was practical experience of driving in a conflict zone and real life knowledge of dealing with the young boisterous type of woman who would be drawn to that type of work. Hers was the experience of an ambulance driver, not of a desk bound administrator who knew what the rule book said on any given subject, but as a driver who had been cold and hungry and had only a tent to look forward to at the end of each day.

Back in Britain, finished with active service, Rotha was appointed Commandant at the British Red Cross motor school. She was made responsible for training ambulance drivers, not only for wartime work, but also for a future peacetime role which came to fruition only after she had left her post at the end of 1918. This was in preparation for the introduction of a service organised jointly between the Red Cross and the Order of St John (St John's Ambulance Brigade), which was a scheme to put in place 500 ambulances stationed and staffed across the entire country. During the war, ambulances had been used simply for transport to medical centres, where medical attention could be delivered. Now civilian ambulances were to be staffed by qualified and trained attendants who could help make sure patients were offered the best attention from initial engagement with the service.

Rotha's address in London was initially given as 41 Elm Park Gardens, where she lived with her mother, and then later as 18 Phillimore Mews, where she lived alone. It was during the period with the Red Cross that Rotha began to fully realise the importance of a uniform for women seeking to retain a sense of importance and status in a society that was beginning to return to pre-war attitudes. Her time with the Red Cross now at an end, she was finally out of uniform, albeit having donned a 'modified' version of the approved SWH attire, replacing skirt with breeches, while in Serbia.

Rotha makes virtually no impact between the end of the war and the early years of the 1920s but by June 1921, when the next census was taken, Rotha had moved down to her grandfather's rural retreat of *Over Langford Manor*, close to Churchill in Somerset, describing herself as a farmer. Rotha has her partner living with her at the farm, thirty-three year old Ethel F. Hill, also from Highgate in London, and unmarried. There is no reason to assume that the description of 'partner' indicates anything other than business partner in the farming business. Also living and working on the farm was Sybil Skelding and a married couple Clarke and Violet Prentice, housekeeper and chauffeur/mechanic.

A picture of life at *Over Langford Manor* is offered by Francis Wookey, who knew Rotha when he was a young child, his father working at the Manor.

> My early recollection of Miss Orman was of a tall, gaunt masculine female - always dressed in an open necked shirt and corduroy breeches, thick long wollen stockings and heavy brown brogue shoes. While at her Langford base she would partake in any job on the farm that was being performed - mucking out the cows and pigs or hay making.[5]

Living at *Over Langford Manor*, life was getting back to normal, Rotha resumed her interest in the scouting and guiding movements, her mother still being heavily involved. She hosted Boy Scout camps on the farm and generally began settling into a traditional rural life.

Meanwhile in London, the Communist Party of Great Britain was organising rallies and demonstrations, while elsewhere articles were appearing which called for the seizing of the means of production and industrial control passing into the hands of the industrial unions. This, under a headline of 'The Dictatorship of the Proletariat and the Building up of Communism'.[6]

The Communist Party of Great Britain had the support of Sylvia Pankhurst, the daughter of Emmeline, who had disagreed with her mother over the 1914 decision to put the suffrage campaign on hold. She had continued campaigning throughout the war and, with the 1917 Russian revolution, rejuvenated the Communist Party of Great Britain with a period of increased political radicalism.

A letter in one of the provincial newspapers offered a portent of what was to come, and pre-empted a thought that Rotha was about to give substance to.

> If only this wretched class distinction could end, and one united effort by all classes made to overcome this present crisis, I think that would be a better solution than the suggestion of Mr G's to overthrow the Capitalist system which could only mean more bloodshed and untold misery . . . I am in no way connected with any capitalists,

> in fact I am only a clerk, many months unemployed, but I fail to realise the advantages of putting into practice the suggestions offered by the Communists to help me to secure employment.[7]

Rotha Lintorn-Orman had much to think upon as she worked on her Somerset farm and tended her vegetable garden. She, like many others, might ask herself if the sacrifices of the First World War were to wither in the peace. Whether the cause of King and Country was to be abandoned in favour of the communist beliefs of Lenin and International Socialism.

*Chapter 9*

# The Rise of Mussolini

A General Election was held in Britain on 15 November 1922, bringing to an end the wartime coalition government that had been in place since 1915. That election was won by the Conservative Party, led by Andrew Bonar Law but, even though victorious, the Conservatives had sustained a net loss of thirty-five seats. Bonar Law's message had been one of continuity, 'tranquillity and stability both at home and abroad so that free scope should be given to the initiative and enterprise of our own citizens'. There was a hint of protectionism in that message, not too dissimilar to one that was widespread among the victorious nations, particularly Italy.

The significance of the result was not that it saw a victory for the Conservative Party, but that this was the first election that had resulted in the Labour Party becoming the principal Opposition party, gaining more seats than the two wings of the Liberal Party combined. The Liberal Party was fairly evenly split into their two factions, and together they suffered a net loss of forty-eight seats. The real winner was the Labour Party under John Robert Clynes, with a net gain of eighty-five seats, and securing over 29 per cent of the popular vote.

Clynes, from an Irish family, was born in Oldham and served in Parliament for some years as a Labour member for various Manchester seats, having first got into politics via his trade union membership. During the First World War he had been in favour of British military involvement, being at odds with Ramsey MacDonald, and in 1921 was appointed leader of the Labour Party. His support for a separate Jewish homeland in Palestine preceded the issuing of the Balfour Declaration by some months.

Rotha Lintorn-Orman's vote was cast in the constituency of Weston-super-Mare where it was a two horse race between John Erskine for the Conservative and Unionist Party, and Frank Murrell for the Liberal Party, although the Liberals were at a disadvantage, their support being split between the Lloyd George and the Asquith factions. Erskine, who was later to become Lord Erskine, was from a military background and destined to eventually join the British Union of Fascists, but in this election chose to label himself as Unionist rather than Conservative, which was an indication of his later views on Home Rule.

Within a month Bonar Law was replaced by Stanley Baldwin, and after another six months John Robert Clynes also stood down in favour of Ramsay MacDonald, in both cases because of ill health. The Palace of Westminster was to became a hotbed of intra-party gossip on both sides. To further complicate matters, the 1922 election had resulted in the introduction of Labour Party intellectuals into Parliament, supplementing the left wing passion of the Trades Union representatives, and allowing them to counter claims of Labour's lower educational achievements.

While those in Westminster may have concerned themselves with parliamentary intrigues and conspiracies, the population at large anticipated the possibility that the next General Election, although not due for some time, could result in a leader of the Labour Party being asked to form a government. Should that happen, then there was the prospect of nationalisation of the railway and of the coal industry, and the possibility of legislation on wage levels and over the standard of housing enjoyed by the working class.

For Rotha Lintorn-Orman, and for her mother, the threat of communism and of the wider acceptance of socialism across Europe, represented a risk to the British way of life and, indirectly, to the future of the British Empire and to British interests. There was a general fear among Conservatives that the sympathies of the working classes were taking hold within the Labour Party; a sympathy that was being fuelled by the disappointment that Britain clearly had not become a 'land fit for heroes'. There was a constant fear that a repeat of what happened in Russia could also happen in Britain.

One of a number of independent members of parliament elected in 1922 was Oswald Mosley. Originally sitting as a Conservative in 1918 Moseley had 'crossed the floor' in 1920 to take his place on the Liberal benches in opposition to the Conservative Government's Irish policy. His objections to the Conservative's backing of the Black and Tans' actions in Ireland during a period of unrest, seems a little at odds with his later support for strong arm tactics employed on the mainland in support of fascism. After 1922 Mosley went on to move ever closer to the left of politics, finally joining the Labour Party in 1924.

The Black and Tans were additional constables recruited specifically to assist the Royal Irish Constabulary (RIC) in the suppression of the IRA and soon gained a reputation for their brutality. The majority were former British soldiers from England, discharged at the end of the First World War, and were now without employment. The Black and Tans became notorious for their reprisal attacks including murder, arson and looting against the Irish civil population and were seen by the Irish as pariahs. The name Black and Tans stems from their uniform of dark blue tunics and caps, and khaki trousers.

Fear of communism was becoming very real in Britain, and those on the right wing of the Conservative Party were conscious of the examples being offered to the British working classes on what political revolution might offer them. Josef Stalin was a rising star in Russia, with Lenin being all but dispossessed of his authority. Lenin had freely admitted that the Soviets could not run the economy but had instead to rely upon forceful compulsion, rather than intellectual persuasion, to convince the population to conform. The country was in the midst of famine, which forced Russia to secretly enter into the Treaty of Rapallo, a pact with Germany that was a contravention of the terms of the 1919 Treaty of Versailles.

The Treaty of Rapallo provided for the complete resumption of diplomatic relations between the Russia and Germany, with both countries foregoing all claims to compensation and both agreeing on a procedure to resolve disputes. Germany accepted Russian nationalisation of German assets in Russia, and waived all other claims, provided that Russia did not acknowledge similar claims from other countries. Germany and Russia each granted the other commercial 'most favoured nation' status and both pledged to promote trade and economic relations between the two countries.

In Germany that pact was viewed with suspicion by the right wing, seeing it as a means by which Bolsheviks and Jewish financiers might conspire together to take effective control of the country. That fear was voiced by Adolf Hitler in August 1922 in a speech to the United Patriotic Associations of Bavaria in Munich, where leaders of other nationalist groups echoed his sentiments. Benito Mussolini expounded similar views in Italy but, unlike Hitler at this time, Mussolini was slightly further down the road to gaining power and establishing the means to 'correct' the situation.

> Internationalization today means only Judaisation. We in Germany have come to this: that a sixty-million people sees its destiny to lie at the will of a few dozen Jewish bankers . . . If families who have lived in Germany for a thousand years are now expropriated, we must do the same to the Jewish usurers . . . we demand immediate expulsion of all Jews who have entered Germany since 1914, and of all those, too, who through trickery on the Stock Exchange or through other shady transactions have gained their wealth.[1]

In Britain, the words of Mussolini were heard as a rallying cry by those fearful of the march of communism. In his 1919 Milan address, Mussolini had spoken of an electoral system based on proportional representation, an assembly to determine whether Italy would remain a monarchy or become a republic, and the proposed suppression of socialist newspapers. He offered a vision of Fascists not only becoming a political force within a parliamentary system, but also being a force on the street, by direct violent action. What commanded the attention of Rotha Beryl Lintorn-Orman was his promise of suffrage for both men and women,[2] a campaign which had been postponed in Britain at the outbreak of war, and which she felt was long overdue for a revival.

Despite the hope that Mussolini's words gave to those still seeking universal suffrage, Italian women would soon become quite disillusioned by the results. Women were finally given the vote in 1925, but only for local elections, and their attempts to form an autonomous group within the Fascist Party in 1924 were frustrated by Mussolini, with a resulting reduction of their influence within the party machine. As time went by, women's role within fascism was redefined as one of simply rearing children to continue the expansion of the fascist cause.

Specifically, the Fascist Manifesto called for the lowering of the voting age, for both men and women, to eighteen but eligibility to hold office be restricted to twenty-five and above. It called for the replacement of the 'upper house' or Senate by an appointed house of experts (labour, industry, transportation, public health, communications, etc.) and that upper house being given legislative powers. It also called for the introduction of an eight hour day, with a statutory minimum wage, and a reduction in the retirement age to fifty-five.

The latter parts of that manifesto found significant support among the working classes in Britain and among the large number of ex-soldiers and sailors who had returned to civilian life in Britain, injured and battle-scarred, without work and without recompense. Their discontent had shown itself in the 'peace day riots' that had taken place in Luton, where the town hall was burnt to the ground, and also in Swindon and Coventry but not with such serious consequences.

An underlying cause of the riot in Luton was the unproven charge that the Mayor and members of the Luton Corporation Food Control Committee profiteered by raising food prices during the war. Regardless of the real reasons for the food shortages and high prices, people blamed the local Food Control Committee. When the local authority then set up a Peace Committee to celebrate the victory, that committee did not involve any of the ex-servicemen's bodies, but announced that a halfpenny rate would be raised to help pay for all celebrations.

> Messrs Farmer & Co.'s piano warehouse . . . was broken into and the instruments dragged into the street. To the tune of 'Keep the Home Fires Burning' the wilder elements of the huge gathering danced and sang, some even mounting a grand piano for the purpose . . . All this time the Brigade maintained its attack on the blaze, the hydrants and hose being guarded by special constables, though the force was sadly depleted, owing to the number of men who had been injured and had been removed for treatment to the police station and to the Bute Hospital . . . Several members of the crowd, including a crippled

> ex-soldier, then mounted the Town Hall steps and impassioned speeches were made, grievances regarding pensions and other matters affecting discharged and disabled men being ventilated.[3]

Rotha Lintorn-Orman, with her family's strong military, rather than commercial, background was not unnecessarily concerned with Mussolini's social reforms but would have been sympathetic to the plight of the returned soldiers and sailors. She was greatly at odds however with the suggestion that the question of monarchy or republic should even be debated, certainly not if that same question should ever be mooted in a British manifesto. Her promises made as a Girl Scout and later as a Girl Guide to King and Country were very sincerely made, and not to be cast aside lightly.

The first seeds of republicanism were already stirring Ireland with the Anglo-Irish Treaty of 1922 being thought of as a possible first step towards that goal. Ireland had already achieved a level of independence from Britain by being granted Dominion status within the British Empire; a concept referred to as 'home rule'. Although Ireland obtained a level of self-determination, the Westminster government retained some military and foreign policy powers.

There had been unrest in Ireland since the civil war had begun in 1919. Irish republican separatists, in the form of the IRA, attacked British troops, police stations, and other targets on the island, ending in conference to end the conflict at which the prospect of the splitting of the island between the Irish Free State and a loyalist Ulster was discussed as a real possibility.

One sticking point was the British insistence that members of the Irish parliament should take an oath of allegiance to the British monarch; a very contentious matter.

After yet more conflict a treaty was finally concluded and the Irish Free State was created in June 1922. This event alone provided a rallying call for the conservative minded upper class who had seen the fall of Russia, and now saw a similar 'rebellion' nearer to home. In the eyes of the Lintorn-Ormans and their circle there was a common theme, the overthrow of the natural order and the imposition of new order; the root cause was International Socialism.

Socialism threatened the status quo that had hitherto existed in the heartland of Britain, and the fear of International Socialism, which was the logical outcome of having a strong Russia, put the British Empire in peril. The consequences for Canada, Australasia and New Zealand, with their very British traditions, were not so much feared as were the effects on the newer, third world countries that might be more easily swayed. The case against socialism was very clear in the minds of the extreme right wing of political thought.

Mussolini's position regarding the Catholic Church was a little more problematical for Rotha who came from a religious family. However, Mussolini's problem with the Church of Rome was to be short lived, once Pope Pius XI came to the view that the Fascists might be his most effective ally against the rising Marxist influence in Italian politics. Even within the church the left wing views of the *Partito Popolare Italiano* were seen as a threat to the Vatican's compromise on the concept of

Catholic social teaching, which itself could be said to be at odds with the Church's well known desire to closely accumulate and hold financial assets, flying in the face of national poverty.

The foundation of Mussolini's movement came from a deep seated belief in socialism for the national good. His nationalism was admired by those in England who were of a similar disposition; his original anti-imperialist views, such as his stand against the colonial war in Libya, being forgiven or ignored. His were not the views of a pacifist, and Mussolini's support for Italy entering the First World War as an ally of Britain, chimed well in the political corridors of London.

> The Austro-German advance into northern Italy led to a genuine outburst of patriotism among ordinary Italians and to keep the soldiers in line the government made many rash promises, including land for the peasants in uniform and the Italian equivalent of Lloyd George's 'homes fit for heroes'. This raised hopes, and when they were not fulfilled after 1918 an ugly mood of resentment developed which could be manipulated by agitators of the left or the right.[4]

In 1922 the British Government was not greatly sympathetic towards the Italian government's difficulties with Mussolini, commenting that the new order proposed may be preferable to the chaos in Italy that pertained. Mussolini's show of patriotism seems to have been something that the British establishment could support. *The Times* newspaper commented:

> The Fascisti are a strange organisation of mixed origin. They are obviously not reactionaries, otherwise they would not have succeeded in withdrawing from Socialist influence such a considerable body of working men. They are intensely patriotic and at the same time, in their popular appeal, they stand for a return to the older creative ideals of Italian Liberalism. Their violence may too easily degenerate into excess, but it can only be understood as a reaction to the subversive forces which are undermining the independent existence of the nation.[5]

By November 1921 Mussolini felt it was a prudent moment for the fascist movement to morph itself into a political party; the *Partito Nazionale Fascista* was formed. As the leader of a recognised political party, Mussolini could play a more traditional role within the existing political framework and reach out to all parts of the Italian public. The advantages of transition, from pressure group to political party, was not lost to those concerned about the perceived communist threat to Britain.

In February of the following year the government of Ivanoe Bonomi collapsed and, after some failed attempts to form minority governments, Mussolini recognised an opportunity to capitalise on the general political disarray. With his heady mixture of nationalism and socialism, both sides of industry working together for the common good, the fascist message offered an end to division and industrial strife. However unpalatable the doctrine of left wing socialism was to swallow, landowners and industrialists were prepared to support Mussolini, not only with words, but with financial contributions.

In Britain, the enthusiasm of Rotha Lintorn-Orman and her like, the strident suffrage troops who had gone through the First World War and were ready to cudgel their way through the peace, saw the direct intervention of the *squadre d'azione* (action squads) as a necessary, if not welcome, avenue of involvement for their pent up energy and commitment. Should a like movement develop in Britain, similar action squads would be needed, but the British proletariat could not be relied upon to support such a radical movement. Such a movement would need to be driven by a different class; the upper class who were accustomed to the military approach to problem solving and who could subvert their own finer feeling to secure the 'greater' good.

In the future, a socialist/liberal backlash could be a possible counterbalance to nationalistic ambitions for Britain; such a backlash was a real and current threat to Mussolini, who decided on a pre-emptive strike by marching on Rome, the seat of government. A number of northern cities had already fallen to the Fascists, the fall of the capital would cement their takeover of the country. However, the threat of a coup d'état by force was sufficient to persuade King Victor Emmanuel III to ask Mussolini to form a new government. Mussolini accepted, announced his cabinet, and orchestrated 70,000 of his uniformed supporters to march through Rome in order to be saluted by the king. The threat of a military coup had been sufficient to achieve a political coup.

*Chapter 10*

# British Patriotism

Despite it being a political coup in Italy the transition was by no means bloodless. In Milan, new found power prompted the now disbanded populist civilian Fascisti to carry out reprisals against the Socialist newspaper *Avanti*, ransacking its offices and making it impossible to continue publishing. Further south, Fascisti en route to Rome were injured by a bomb left under a seat in one of the train carriages in which they were travelling. The revenge was quick and devastating, sacking and burning all the communist properties in the nearby town of Bari, with street fighting breaking out in the wider area.[1]

Those on the far right wing of British politics saw, in Mussolini, someone taking a practical step forward in countering the Bolshevik drive towards undermining the established European way of life and threatening its commercial institutions. For this breakdown they blamed a coalition of Jewish financiers and Russian communists who had first destabilised pre-war Germany and was now attempting to deliver a similar fate to Italy, that is until Mussolini had put a stop to their plans by direct action. Belief was that Germany's defeat in the First World War had put an end to its ambition of defeating the British Empire on the way to world domination by a German-Jewish-Bolshevik cabal.

In Britain views on Mussolini began to be disputed within the liberal press that regularly printed reports of how bad the conditions were in Italy, in the main from newspapers such as the *Daily Chronicle* and the *Daily News*, portraying life as dangerous both for the dissenter, and for the individual. Whether their comments about life under Mussolini were right or wrong, their predictions for the short-term life of his regime proved to be incorrect which, in turn, led to their argument being held as flawed.

> The Fascisti of Rome this afternoon paraded for the taking of the Fascist oath before Signor Mussolini, who afterwards reviewed the men and exhorted them to work and keep discipline for the greatness and the restoration of Italy. Then they marched past the tomb of the Unknown Soldier to the Quirinal, where they gave cheers for the King and Queen, who came out on to one of the palace balconies to bow [sic] their thanks, before dispersing they made a similar demonstration in front of the Queen-Mother's residence.[2]

The more traditional members of the Conservative Party were less critical of Mussolini's Italy than were the liberal newspapers. There were those in influential positions, as well as the rank and file, who ignored the detailed reports of what was happening to dissenters in Italy simply because the dissenter was, in all probability, a socialist or a communist, and such people were out to undermine the very principles of the pre-war established order. In the view of those in the pro-Mussolini camp, the danger came from socialists or communists, not from the Fascists.

Of those expounding such views, Alan Ian Percy the 8th Duke of Northumberland, was probably the most vocal. He owned the Boswell Printing and Publishing Company and, attracting readers such as Rotha Lintorn-Orman, began publishing *The Patriot* on 9 February 1922. One of its main contributors was Nesta Webster whose anti-Semitic views were to be found in the majority of her writings, blaming Jewish conspiracies for much of recent history's calamities including the French Revolution, the First World War, and the Bolshevik Revolution. Most pertinent to Britain was blaming the current popularity of Ramsay MacDonald, in order to malign Jewish socialist influence.

The first edition was very much the work of Alan Percy himself, writing not only the mission statement but also the 'leader' and many of the other articles.

> The Patriot has been started for a trial period of three months, for the purpose of supplying briefly striking facts and arguments relating to movements threatening the safety and welfare of the British Empire; movements, the dangers of which are either concealed or made light of in the majority of the newspapers. The public generally have been kept in ignorance for several years, through what appears to be a concerted policy between a section of the Government and an influential portion of the Press, both swayed by alien influences hostile to the Nation. There is no intention of producing the

> ordinary news of the established newspapers; but it is proposed simply to publish details omitted by nearly all of them, and yet of vital importance to the proper understanding of movements and tendencies below the surface of events.[3]

In that first edition Lord Sydenham of Combe wrote on the unrest in India, describing the Indians as an illiterate, excitable, and a credulous people, and a seething mass of incongruous elements over which the firm rule of Britain has hitherto maintained peace. Nesta Webster wrote of the dilution of the conservative message, the concept rather than party, and that the 1905 Aliens Act had protected the working man's means of earning a living; an Act that had been opposed by the parliamentary Liberal Party.

Lord Sydenham of Combe, otherwise known as Sir George Sydenham Clarke, was already an old man when *The Patriot* was first launched by Alan Percy in 1922. After a successful military career he served as Governor of Victoria in Australia, and then as Governor of Bombay in India. He was described as '. . . an insensitive, clumsy, uncouth and infinitely boring man . . .' by one biographer. He held strong anti-Semitic views which were expressed in a number of publications including *The Britons*, a leading anti-immigration magazine. Sir George Sydenham Clarke, with a similar background as Sir Lintorn Simmons, was certainly in the same social circle as Blanch Lintorn-Orman, and held similar political opinions.

Nesta Webster argued that Bolshevism was part of a much older and more secret conspiracy and that the *Protocols of the*

*Elders of Zion*, even if false, still described how Jews behaved. She favoured 'traditional roles for women', but saw marriage as limiting women's choices for education, and that the education they did receive was inferior to that of men's. She favoured women being allowed to vote and favoured keeping the British Parliamentary system for the benefit of both men and women. This latter point satisfied the young suffragettes that were attracted to her notions.

The theme of protectionism was a common one found in the Italian model of fascism and that ethos was proclaimed by this new *Patriot* publication. The 1905 Act introduced the concept of government controlled immigration measures designed, in this instance, to control Jewish immigration from Eastern Europe, a step that Winston Churchill opposed on the grounds that it would 'appeal to insular prejudice against foreigners, to racial prejudice against Jews, and to labour prejudice against competition'. In 1919 the original Act was revised such that it virtually ended Jewish immigration to Britain.

> The crowd of unemployed that recently marched on a West End restaurant and demanded the expulsion of all foreigners employed there were for once acting on their own initiative, and not on the alien enemies who control the International Socialists' Club. . . Socialists are very anxious to dissociate themselves from Communists. But wherein do they differ? Only in degree and method. . . If Conservatism would but realise that in the working-classes of this country lies its strongest support. . . If

> Conservatives will but make of their political doctrines a living creed they will prevail.[4]

Elsewhere there was much attention paid to the ongoing problems in Ireland, including a proposed treaty between the new Republic of Ireland and the Russian Soviet Republic, one of the aims being the liberation of all people from 'imperialistic exploitation'. Other articles included the growing influence of the Labour Party, co-operatives in general, and the unenviable state of British agriculture; an issue that would provide a launching pad for an East Anglian campaign some years into the future.

> Direct taxation in other industries is passed on to the consumer, but this is not possible with agriculture, for the prices of agricultural products are fixed in relation to foreign importations. This heavy taxation, both imperial and local, is one of the great causes of depression in agriculture and of unemployment in rural districts.[5]

On 4 October 1922, a few days after Mussolini's symbolic march on Rome, members of the London branch of Italian Fascists held their own parade. Previous attempts to march had been frustrated by the Home Office but, with Mussolini now heading a new government, they were no longer seen as marginal to main stream politics. The march made its way past the Cenotaph in Whitehall to Westminster Abbey, where it was received by Bishop Ryle, the Dean of the Abbey; the presence of flag-bearing black shirted marchers kneeling before the Cenotaph while giving the fascist salute, being somewhat incongruous to the surroundings from a modern perspective.

In Britain, *The Times* reminded its readers that Mussolini had threatened the destruction of the British Empire, that the *Fascisti* were aggressive and assertive and established public order in their own way, and that Mussolini had demanded the establishment of a fascist state. More worrying was that Mussolini had threatened that unless the fascists are able to control the Italian government they might take it by force; something that was emphasised by him referring to the Army as an 'ally of the Fascists', prompting calls upon Italian officers to not forget their oath of allegiance.

Another view of Mussolini was also being expressed in the British newspapers. Sir Percival Phillips saw it as 'the rescue of Italy from the cruel despotism of the Bolsheviks and Communists', as the 'Salvation of Italy' and as being 'full of hope and instruction for the world'.[6] These were sentiments shared by many, but far from a majority, of the British population. One person who did share those sentiments was Rotha Lintorn-Orman.

Rotha's mother's circle of friends seems to have included many of those people who would be naturally drawn towards an organisation which supported the aims and ambitions of the Italian Fascisti but with a distinctly British emphasis. There is little evidence to suggest that any organised grouping would have followed Mussolini's interpretation of fascism at this point. At this juncture it was a return to the old and traditional form of conservatism that was being called for, not a foreign manufactured philosophy.

The worries and concern of the day, amongst the traditional conservative supporter, were those of loyalty and patriotism, of the future of the British Empire and, above all, the alienation of any Socialist, Communist or Bolshevik threat on British soil. The old soldiers who were part of Blanch Lintorn-Orman's circle were not seeking a new philosophy, but a return to an old way of life. They were interested in the British Empire, but they were more interested in keeping Socialism at bay, and stopping it from destroying their 'Little England' lifestyle.

The discontent and concern felt in Britain about the decline in patriotism, and the consequent rise of socialism, communism and internationalism, also found a voice regarding the machinations going on in Ireland. The Irish Free State was established as a dominion of the British Empire, which gave it much the same status as held by Canada. The 1921 Anglo-Irish Treaty, which brought the Irish Free State into being, was opposed by both the pro-republican Irish and the loyalists in Ulster and London.

For those in Ireland who were pro-republican, the retention of King George V as head of state of the new dominion was seen as a failure by the IRA in securing full independence, such that the requirement to take an Oath of Allegiance prevented Sinn Féin from taking their seats on the Dáil, a situation that continued for some years. Many members of the Conservative and Unionist Party were quite vocal in their disappointment that the Irish Free State had come into being.

> England confronted with a reunited (even if only temporarily) Ireland will have to decide immediately two questions, the reconquest of Ireland or peace with Ireland . . . England has to choose between holding on to Ulster as a catspaw against the rest of Ireland or surrendering the bridgehead of the North as a base against the South.[7]

In that same edition of *The Patriot* there was a lengthy piece warning of plans, by what the newspaper referred to as the 'Militant Movement', to provoke a revolution in England with the *Daily Herald* at its centre. The article warned of a left wing 'intelligence unit' with its spies everywhere, including within Government offices and the Civil Service Unions collecting and sharing such information with adherents of Socialism and Communism, including Sinn Féin, claiming that the latter was in close contact with the Russian Bolshevist Government.

The choice of the *Daily Herald* as the target of Alan Ian Percy's ire was founded simply on its support for the labour movement. The *Daily Herald* had a chequered history and in 1922 was entering its third phase or manifestation, under the guidance of Hamilton Fyfe, but this time it was the official organ of the Trade Union Congress, albeit read by a cross section of the population. There seems to have been some justification for Percy's mistrust of the *Daily Herald* as there was some evidence of it being in receipt of substantial funding from the Russian Government, although there is no independent confirmation of this.

Elsewhere in Britain there was some social dissatisfaction in agricultural circles, initially within the land owning classes who found that they were prohibited from increasing farm rents because of the Corn Production Act of 1917. Many land owners decided to sell their tenant farms rather than continue with depressed rents. Many tenant farmers felt pressured to purchase their farms, rather than give up on land their families had tended for years, taking on mortgages which they could ill afford. It was estimated that between 1918 and 1920 ten per cent of agricultural land had been purchased by sitting tenants, which had the effect of reducing the average size of each free standing farm close to the point of becoming economically unviable.

The situation was made worse by the Board of Agriculture acquiring 65,000 acres to establish smallholdings for ex-servicemen. Such mini-farms were not really viable, certainly not for de-mobbed men with no financial reserves, and little or no agricultural experience. The situation was further worsened as the availability of agricultural produce from overseas increased, particularly ham and bacon from the United States, the salting process alone providing preservation for the long sea voyage.

By 1923 agriculture was in bad straits; farm gate prices were depressed as a consequence of cheap imports, agricultural wages were as low as 25s per week which meant that workers began drifting away from the land. A further cost against the small farmer, one which very few had anticipated, was the tithe charge, otherwise referred to as the rent charge. Historically the tithe was payable to the Church but, following the dissolution of the monasteries in the sixteenth century, the right to collect tithes had passed to new beneficiaries. For tenant farmers this had been included by the land owner, in the rent, now it fell to the new small land owner to pay the tithe, without any idea as to why.

Although tithe payments were an issue of contention among the new landed farmers, there was little indication of that general feeling developing into an organised opposition. But while the general discontent was not brought to a head in 1922, it was something that would prove a useful tool for the fascist cause in later years, and be used to capture the countryside dwellers, while other campaigns would be proffered in the industrial cities.

It is pertinent to mention here that the mobilisation of farmers and agricultural workers, whilst not brought to a head in the twenties, was very much a fascist issue a decade later. Farmers who couldn't or wouldn't pay the tithe demands faced court action which led to bailiffs being called upon to execute distraint orders, seizing stock and machinery. Such visits were often accompanied by protests from local farmers and their workers, noisy but not given to violence. When stock and machinery were later brought to auction, local farmers, who would normally be expected to bid, were silent and often there would be no sales from an entire farm auction. Police attended such events but they were called upon to do very little.

The fascist view was that if farmers had a guaranteed home market and fair prices then they would be able to double agricultural production levels, and if manufactured industrial imports were also banned in favour of domestic production, the increased purchasing power of full employment would solve the problems of inflation. The fascists also insisted that international financers profited from the chaos created by Communism and war scares and that they should be further controlled.

Little has been mentioned so far about anti-Semitic feelings in the country as a whole but in the main this early manifestation of what is referred to as fascism was not heavily influencing the anti-Semitic debate. There were individuals within the broad spectrum of opinion that saw the Bolsheviks and Germans as being assisted in their schemes by the money-lenders, but that has always been so. It has been socialism and communism that has become the enemy, not the means by which they fight the war.

There were individual members of the group, generally coalescing around Rotha, that definitely held anti-Semitic views, particularly Alan Ian Percy the 8th Duke of Northumberland, who also possessed the only right wing journal, *The Patriot*, through which their views could find their way to print. To assume that the entire group supported every aspect of Alan Percy's creed would be an error.

As 1923 dawned, so did the awareness of a certain faction within the Conservative Party that there was an opportunity to influence the next generation of British society. Mussolini offered one solution for Italy, but not necessarily one that was suitable for Britain in every detail. The British Empire was under threat from Socialism, as was a united Ireland, as was British agriculture having to fight internationalism. The common enemy behind all these threats was Communism, and people like Rotha Lintorn-Orman believed they held the solution.

*Chapter 11*

# A Cadre of Patriots

Upon her return from Serbia and Greece, and following her short period with the Red Cross in London, Rotha opted to live a quieter life in the rural confines of Lower Langford Manor in and around Churchill in Somerset; the Simmons country seat. Still recovering from her illness, perhaps a period spent farming would serve her better than any stylish London clinic, although the energy that she brought to her new pursuit was again extreme. Considering her underlying nature, the total commitment she applied to farming was quite in keeping.

The influence that Blanch Lintorn-Orman exercised over her daughter cannot be overestimated during those early days of peace. Rotha had returned from Serbia unwell, with possible recurring episodes of malaria, so a prolonged period of convalescence would be to her advantage. When she first returned from Serbia the war had not yet concluded, and Rotha was still 'under arms', but once the First World War was over she reverted to being Blanch's daughter once more, with all the connotations of the maternal influence that Blanch exercised.

By the time of the 1921 census it would appear that Rotha's mother and father had decided to live apart, he in shared accommodation in Earls Court, she with her own establishment in Chelsea, complete with live-in staff. Whereas Blanch had the benefit of her father's fortune and was able to maintain her own household, Charles was living as a single man alone in an apartment building.

With Rotha living at Over Langford Manor, inherited by her mother, it seems safe to assume that mother and daughter were still on good terms, an assumption that is borne out by future events. Father and daughter appear not to be so, perhaps as a result of Rotha's lifestyle and her increasing adoption of masculine ways. Perhaps her changing political views and her growing admiration for Mussolini, and her support for his fascist ideology, were at odds with her father's beliefs.

It's not clear why Blanch and Charles were not living together at this time, but a reasonable view would be that the two held very different views regarding the danger that socialism and communism represented to the British way of life, but more particularly the solution that Blanch proposed; one that supported Mussolini's method of dealing with the problem. Blanch, a product of the minor aristocracy; Charles from a more modest background with no land assets to protect. What assets the Linton-Ormans had were firmly held by Blanch, assets that were in danger of being wasted on a useless political venture.

Annie Burley's apartment house at 49 Eardley Crescent was one residence in a row of elegant town houses in Earls Court, that had presented a picture of wealth and achievement before the war, but were now put to a more mundane purpose. As well as Charles Lintorn-Orman, who was identified as a retired major in the British Army, most of the other residents were single or widowed. Only Charles appears to be married, yet living apart from his wife, such an arrangement not viewed as being customary in the 1920s.

Blanch Lintorn-Orman lived at 71 Elm Park Gardens in Chelsea, a substantial private house. Her staff consisted of a lady's maid, a cook and a housemaid. Charles and Blanch were living a little over a mile from one another. John G. Hope, in his book *Surveillance or collusion? Maxwell Knight, MI5 and the British Fascisti*, states that Blanch and Rotha were friends of both Nesta White and Alan Ian Percy, the Duke of Northumberland and founder of *The Patriot*; also friends were Lord and Lady Sydenham of Combe; all admirers of Benito Mussolini.

During the First World War, the two major industries of coal production and the national rail network, while not nationalised, were operated under strict government control. Following the war, and in response to the impending economic depression, there was pressure from the owners to impose wage cuts on the employees of these two industries. The coalition government, under Lloyd-George, resisted this pressure through fear of union strikes, the Transport Workers, Railwaymen, and Miners having entered into a triple alliance to counter any such proposal.

Post war, the Government, owners and miners had to face a re-adjustment within the industry. The demands of the war economy had given rise to a period of inflation and it was assumed that coal prices would continue rising with the export markets for coal re-opening. The mine owners wanted to reap the benefits of victory over Germany, but the coal miners did not want to lose the wage increases that they had seen. Mr Justice Sankey, leading the Sankey Commission, called for nationalisation of the entire coal industry.

The ultra-conservative group coalescing around the Lintorn-Ormans saw, in the industrial action both threatened and taken, that the spectre of socialism as a very real danger. Moreover they saw it as the first indication that the Bolshevik threat from Russia was being exported to Britain and that the time had come to counter that threat. The national wage agreement was at the centre of the coal crisis. The miners refused to abandon the national agreement; the mine owners argued that pits in the less profitable coalfields could not afford existing wage rates. Negotiations were at an impasse.

Finally, following some in-fighting and disagreements between the unions, the Government felt safe in imposing wage cuts on the miners in April 1921. Despite fears to the contrary there were no strikes as a direct consequence, but the Transport Workers and Railwaymen did refuse to handle imported coal. Things were tense for a time but finally the decision not to strike came on Friday, 15 April and that day was generally referred to as 'Black Friday'. Although isolated industrial action did take place later, a general strike was averted, for the time being.

It was some time after 'Black Friday', and as a response to the further threat of industrial action, that the next step towards a solution was taken. The story generally proffered is that Rotha Lintorn-Orman was weeding her kitchen garden at Over Langford Manor when she had an 'epiphany', or a 'road to Damascus', moment, realising that it was up to patriots like her to save Britain from those with left wing views and left wing alliances. She placed an advertisement in *The Patriot* seeking 'prospective anti-syndicalists', by which she meant those opposed to industry-wide trade unionism.

The flaw is the notion that Rotha would have conceived and executed this plan in isolation, suddenly and without consultation or moral support. It is much more likely that Rotha was presented as the figurehead of the movement to come, and that the most likely scenario involves Blanch's circle of friends appointing Rotha as the driving force, as long as Blanch's money was there to finance her. This interpretation is borne out by the fact that any new organisation would not be run by Rotha, but by a group of men, many drawn from the ranks of Blanch's circle of friends.

Such friends and relations were potential supporters of Blanch's own political views and would be willing recruits to her daughter's own political ambitions. Blanch's home in Chelsea offered a suitable venue for mother and daughter to canvass support amongst the 'establishment', and Blanch's fortune could make any plans financially viable. It was this that convinced Rotha to take the next step, and it's impossible to believe that this was not a joint project of mother and daughter.

A number of versions exist regarding the next step taken by Rotha and Blanch in seeking support for their political ambitions. Unfortunately, no copy of *The Patriot* journal exists for the particular editions that carried Rotha's advertisements. Examining other editions of The Patriot it's more likely that Rotha's advertisements were, in fact, letters to the editor, which would have been published in the correspondence section of the journal.

Various suggestions have been offered as to the exact wording of Rotha's appeal to the public, but the phrase 'Seeking Anti-Communists' is the most often offered, and this focuses on her true feeling that Britain was being ruined by foreigners and communists who could only be stopped by using decisive action to overturn the outdated commitment to liberal democracy. There is no suggestion that her desire was to overthrow the British Government, but instead to ensure that the views of the patriotic right were heard and understood.

The result of the response to her call for support was that Rotha was able to bring a cohort of like-minded people together to form the British Fascisti (BF) as an ultra-conservative paramilitary organisation. Rotha's hand on the structure of the new pressure group can be seen in its early adoption of the idea of a uniform, and its pseudo militaristic structure. Some observers likened the new group to the Boy Scout movement, no doubt a negative reference to both Rotha's and Blanch's early association with that, and subsequent, movements such as the Girl Guides.

This insistence on drawing a parallel between the newly formed BF and the boy scout movement relies on the premise that Rotha used the name 'Fascisti' while not fully understanding the true nature of fascism. A more plausible explanation would be that Rotha and her conservative friends used a term which had not properly been defined at that time and therefore was available as a name for ultra-conservatism, which the BF really represented.

It is relevant to note that the term 'fascist' was not used until 1915 and not in wider use until 1919 when Mussolini founded the Italian *Fasces of Combat* in Milan, which used the name 'Fascisti' only in 1921. Historians and political scientists have all defined fascism in terms of what it has meant in retrospect, rather than as a pre definition term against which any new movement could be tested. The name 'fascist' comes from the ancient Roman fasces, a bundle of rods tied around an axe, suggesting strength through unity; a single unit is easily broken, whereas a bundle is much stronger.

Early members of the BF were drawn, largely, from the middle and upper classes, all of whom were associated with the Conservative Party, joining the new group but staying within that political party, seeing this new organisation as being an extension to their existing loyalties. In the eyes of the founding members, there was no conflict of interest between the two movements; one was a pressure group within the other.

One such recruit was Viscountess Lady Downe, born Dorothy Ffolkes at Hillington Hall, near King's Lynn in Norfolk, and still plain Mrs Dawney at this point. Dorothy Dawney, like Rotha, had also spent the war in a medical or para-medical role, serving as commandant of the Royal Flying Corps Auxiliary Hospital at Hillington Hall, her family home. She and her husband also handed over Wykeham Abbey, his family seat in Yorkshire, to the Red Cross for use as a recovery hospital for non-commissioned officers and soldiers, and it's estimated that more than 1,500 men passed through the Abbey during the war.

Dorothy Dawney saw no reason why it should be thought of as strange that she should belong to both groups. After all, the BF sought only to re-state the basic tenet of the Conservative Party – support for the established order; no question of establishing a new order. Preservation of the British Empire, and loyalty to the Royal Family in the face of possible calls for a Republic could not be regarded as being at odds with conservatism.

Nesta Helen Webster, referred to previously, subscribed to the view that *The Illuminati*, in league with the Jews, Masons and Jesuits, were plotting a communist takeover of the world. The embodiment of the defunct eighteenth century secret society, *The Illuminati*, within a twentieth century Communist plot to take over the world, was laughable, and certainly played no part in Rotha's own political campaigning. Webster was a contributor to The Jewish Peril series of *Morning Post* articles and was a major contributor to Alan Percy's journal *The Patriot,* that Rotha had used to curry support, and was well thought of by the British Freemasons; foreign Freemasons were considered by Nesta to be subversive.

Webster's overriding obsession appears to have been with the Jews, describing them as having a 'lust for gain at the price of human suffering'; unlike Rotha who seems to show little interest in the Jews except to the extent that their interests were seen to converge with those of the Communists. Webster, unlike many women who joined the BF, was never part of the suffrage movement although she was in favour of women's suffrage. Her refusal to join the movement was due to her not believing that simply having the vote would lead to equality with men, rather that men's view of women would not change until men and women had the same educational opportunities.

She, like Rotha, was dismayed at the signing of the Treaty of Rapallo between Russia and Germany, which engendered even stronger anti-German feelings in her. Outside her own group of like-minded followers, Nesta's writings were not widely endorsed or accepted.

> She is one of those people who have got one cause on the brain. It is the good old 'Jewish revolutionary' bogey. But there is a type of unstable mind which cannot rest without morbid imaginings, and the conception of a single cause simplifies thought. With this good woman it is the Jews, with some people it is the Jesuits, with others Freemasons and so on.[1]

One of the men to join the BF in the early days was Robert Byron Drury Blakeney, often referred to as General Blakeney although his final rank was Brigadier-General. It was Blakeney, later to become Rotha's nemesis, who was to liken the BF to an adult version of the Boy Scouts, with its principles of fraternity, duty and service, and insisting that it be run on the basis of a 'spirit of intelligent patriotism'.

Arnold Leese, a prominent veterinarian and specialist in the care of camels, joined the BF at its formation. During the war he had served in the Royal Army Veterinary Corps and after the armistice settled in Stamford, Lincolnshire where he went into private practice. Leese was an admirer of Benito Mussolini and was naturally drawn to the prospect of an Italian style fascist movement in Britain.

Leese, not being London-centric, was one of the first to create a provincial branch, successfully standing for election to Stamford Town Council under the banner of the BF; likewise Harry Simpson, a fellow branch member. The Stamford branch soon grew to eighty members but Leese was opposed to the Fascisti allowing Jews and 'former' socialists to join, as he feared the entire movement to be 'honeycombed' with communists. Leese was, like Nesta Webster, an anti-Semite, becoming more vocal on the subject as time went by, and finally leaving to form his own anti-Semitic group.

Early recruits were not exclusively from the middle or upper classes. William Joyce, later to be known as 'Lord Haw Haw', was one of those who could be relied upon to use his fists in support of the cause. Joyce was born in New York to Irish parents, returning to Ireland when he was nine years old and then to England at fourteen. When his association with the BF began he was only seventeen years old and it was during this time that he was attacked and left with a facial scar for the rest of his life.

The *Daily Herald* published a front page article announcing to its readership the formation of the BF and expressing its concerns over the dangers of such an anti-Socialist organisation. The piece quotes a circular printed by Alan Percy's company and gives Blanch Lintorn-Orman's address as that for the BF's office. The *Daily Herald* described *The Patriot* as devoted to 'Jew baiting' and 'misrepresenting Socialism'. According to the *Daily Herald*, their legal experts considered the organisation to be illegal, setting up as a rival to the police and military forces.

The following day the same newspaper published what it described as the 'Enrolment Oath', warning that a similar fascist structure existed at the outset of Mussolini's campaign in Italy, and that this movement was an attempt to overthrow progressive elements within Great Britain.

> In the name of God I solemnly swear to uphold His Most Gracious King George V, his heirs and successors, and the British Empire. I understand that, without personal consideration, I will render every service within my power to the British Fascisti in their struggle against all treacherous and revolutionary movements now working for the destruction of the Throne and Empire.[2]

Rotha's hand can be clearly seen again in the construction of the Oath, in its simplicity and in its naivety. Not dissimilar to the original 1908 Boy Scout's Promise: 'On my honour I promise that I will do my duty to God and the King: I will do my best to help others, whatever it costs me: I know the scout law, and will obey it'. Criticism of Rotha seems most often to reflect upon her Girl Guide approach to politics and to her lack of understanding as to the true nature of Mussolini's fascist movement.

Even at this very early stage, Rotha had drawn the attention of the security services in the form of Maxwell Knight, a young MI5 agent who was directed to infiltrate the BF movement. It was Knight, appointed as Director of Intelligence for the BF, who then detailed members to infiltrate British communist groups. Knight had been introduced to MI5 by Sir George McGill, who ran a private intelligence agency. McGill and his deputy were early followers of Rotha's movement, describing her as 'one of the bravest people I have ever met'.

Other early members included Neil Francis Hawkins, E. G. Mandeville Roe, Lady Sydenham of Combe, Lady Menzies of

Menzies and Baroness Zouche of Haryneworth. These early recruits seemed to be drawn from a social group who were not linked only by class, but appeared to be known to one another, forming a larger network; the common denominator of which was Blanch Lintorn-Orman.

*Chapter 12*

# Speeches & Pamphlets

British newspapers had been largely enthusiastic that Italy was going down a road that would lead to more certainty and continuity. Previously, the country had no clear leader, but Mussolini's appointment as the Italian Premier promised some level of confidence for the future. Whatever the political leanings of individual newspapers, there were very clear concerns about the levels of violence which accompanied the uniformed gatherings. While accepting Italy's move towards fascism, the newspapers were less than enthusiastic about the risk of accompanying Italian style violence reaching the streets of Britain.

> The rise of Italian Fascism was certainly viewed with interest by political commentators in Britain . . . Mussolini's movement was somehow introducing 'order' to counter and reverse revolutionary 'chaos', and that this could only be a good and positive development . . . The Italian Fascist creed was mainly treated in a stereotypical way as a rather exotic and very unrestrained solution, a typical product of southern Mediterranean 'hot tempers', a 'foreign' creed unsuited to the supposedly calm English temperament. At the same time, many British politicians quietly approved of the Italian leader's destruction of Bolshevism.[1]

The early days of the BF (British Fascisti) was a period in which a practical structure began to develop, in organisational terms, if not in political or ideological terms. The lack of a proper understanding of Fascist ideology, particularly the Italian version, was a criticism that would follow Rotha through the following years. An early development was to appoint Lord Garvagh as president of the nine strong Fascist Grand Council and below that, an executive council which oversaw a series of functional units such as transport and propaganda.

Lord Garvagh's home was in Ireland and he was not able to take any day-to-day position within BF, but rather saw himself fulfilling the purely symbolic role of president. Correctly named Leopold Ernest Stratford George Canning, he was able to bring together an array of military men to form the Fascist Grand Council including Sir Arthur Henry Hardinge, who had been a senior British diplomat during the war years.

During the first year of its existence the BF, while being the inspirational product of Rotha's ambition to protect the patriotic principles held by the Conservative Party, and frustrate the plans of an insidious left wing cabal, were not rallied by her personal charisma. With no strong leader the movement concentrated on those things that it fought against, with no singular policy of what it actually strove to achieve. The result was uncertainty, both of direction and of intended final outcome.

Lord Garvagh was not entirely committed to long term involvement with the movement and in 1924 gave way to Robert Byron Drury Blakeney, previously referred to as General Blakeney who, at the same time took over as editor of *The Fascist Bulletin*, the organisation's own journal. One of Blakeney's first actions was to change the group's Italian sounding name from 'British Fascisti' to 'British Fascists', seen as an appeasement to the notion of British patriotism, a sign that the group was anxious to distance itself from some of the more distasteful developments in Italy.

Like Rotha, Blakeney's understanding of the ideology was of his own making, not that of later, more high profile fascists. His contribution at this stage was firstly to press for a more militaristic structure for the BF, introducing a rigid line of command. Secondly to change its name to the more English sounding 'British Fascist', so severing any ideas of having links to a foreign organisation.

Blakeney ideology was one of ultra-conservatism and the BFs must be ready to defend established society in the event that 'the swarms from the slums' are persuaded to revolt as they had in Russia. He also believed that the Italian model could not simply be applied to Britain as the British worker was less prone to communism than were the Italians. The name change was testament to such a contention, his aim being to present a British movement both in name and in ethos which he could not do with the Italian sounding name 'Fascisti'.

Despite Rotha's sympathies with the cause of women's suffrage, the structure of the BF under Blakeney was soon divided into two sections; a main section which was primarily the domain of men, and a secondary women's unit which was entirely the province of women. Rotha managed to remain at the heart of the organisation, most probably because it was her mother's fortune that financed the day-to-day operations.

Although Rotha was an integral member of the Fascist Grand Council, first under the chairmanship of Lord Garvagh and then General Blakeney, she took a keen interest in the women's unit, particularly the work they were doing with young people by way of the Fascist Children's Clubs.

> The Children's Clubs were created in 1925, and by March 1926 the Assistant Director of Women's Units was reporting that around forty had been set up with a total membership of almost 3,000. 'We started teaching them to salute the Flag, and then got busy on games', one article reported, noting 'the look of happiness on every child's face, as they went away fortified with a stick of Fascist rock or an orange'.[2]

The Fascist Children's Club also published pamphlets, in which Rotha took a particular interest, one of which bears her name as author. *The Red Menace to British Children* is more concerned with the fear of socialist influence on education than it is in promoting a fascist alternative. She fears a loss of 'Love of Country' which she sees as a reflection of the 'apathy and indifference of the post-war British citizen' and blames two subversive movements; the Bolsheviks and the Occult.

Her attack on the Bolsheviks is fairly straightforward in that she cites the Socialist Sunday Schools as recruiting its teachers from Conscientious Objectors, trained while being interned at Dartmoor during the war years. There may be some truth in her claim in that of the 1,000 Conscientious Objectors confined in Dartmoor Prison many were 'anarchists, and preachers of a bastard socialism' and had strong political allegiances to the Communist Party although no evidence of Sunday School training.

The BF relied on there being a growing fear of a Bolshevik revolution in the wings of mounting industrial unrest within British industry. A fear that was nurtured by the BF, aided and abetted by some sections of the right wing press, particularly the *Daily Mail* and its publication of the Zinoviev letter. The letter was entirely false but purported to be from the head of Communist International, to the head of the British Communist Party, saying that if the Labour Party were to be elected it would be in a perfect position to promote a revolution.

Her criticism of the Communist Sunday Schools was even more stern, accusing them of penetration by stealth into the Socialist Sunday Schools in order to lead those schools even further to the left. Rotha went on to list 'Red' organisations that had a 'lamentable' effect on children, including the Young Socialist League, the ILP Guild of Youth, the Young Communist International and the Red Boy Scouts and Girl Guides who 'pervert the clean and patriotic ideals of scouting'.

The Young Socialist League was formed in 1911 with strong connections to the Socialist Sunday Schools but had merged with the Young Labour League in 1921 to form the Young Workers' League, a forerunner of the Young Communist League, the youth section of the British Communist Party. Similarly the ILP Guild of Youth was the youth section of the Independent Labour Party formed in 1924.

In a second pamphlet *Communist Sunday Schools*, Rotha discusses the Bill that was going through Parliament to counter seditious and blasphemous teaching to children. She of course supported the Bill, using the opportunity to attack the Communists, claiming that they 'couple atheism and revolution because they know that in the destruction of the Christian faith they break down one of the greatest of the barriers standing for law and order'. She claims that the Communist Sunday Schools, held secretly in private houses, promoted the idea of revolution in Britain and encouraged children to reject any idea of patriotism.

The Duke of Atholl, speaking in the Lords and recorded by Hansard had the following to say on the Bill:

> I have in my hand a book called Manual for Leaders of Children's Groups . . . one of the standard books of the Communist Sunday Schools . . . published by the Young Communist International . . . contains a good deal with regard to sex education - how to train children and send them off for long rambles together, so that they may teach each other . . . to disobey their teachers and their parents, so that they may be ready for the revolution which is coming . . . urges children on to rebellion and to immorality . . . urges children to do what they can against the police.

Rotha reserved her most severe judgement for the members of the occult groups that, in her view, preached an anti-Christian and anti-British message. She believed that the very fact that these occult organisations were 'international' was, in itself, proof that they were anti-British and should be banned entirely. Amongst the most notorious groups that Rotha considered subversive was the Kibbo Kift Kindred which had pagan rites, totem poles and the cult of nudity at its root, along with their practicing pseudo Masonic rites.

This Kibbo Kift Kindred, begun by John Hargrave a Quaker and pacifist of Jewish Hungarian descent, was a little eccentric in its beliefs and ways. He believed that the individual, strengthened by self-discipline, was the future of mankind, rather than group action based upon race, class or nationality. There was a strong social, as opposed to socialist, element to its beliefs, but its belief in an internationalist future was at odds with Rotha's fascist views. Hargrave's belief in taking inspiration from the woodcraft ideas of Ernest Thompson Seton was also a significant stumbling block.

The occult dimension to Hargrave's ideas, manifesting itself in a fondness for symbolism, art and ritual was too difficult to reconcile with the ambitions of the fascist cause. His woodcraft name was White Fox, and he organised woodland camps for devotees where they dressed in costume, increasing over time to take on a more ceremonial rather than woodland appearance. The Kibbo Kift Kindred employed a terminology quite alien to everyday English and the introduction of symbols such as regalia and totem poles distanced it even further from the main stream.

Rotha's dislike of the occult puts her diametrically opposite the later Nazi obsession with the supernatural, particularly noticeable in Adolf Hitler's behaviour during the 1939–1945 war. Here again the Nazis looked back to an ancient Indian symbol to rally around just as the Italian fascist did around the ancient Roman 'fasces'. It is worth noting that the BF used only the monogram 'F' on their paraphernalia.

Other occult organisations were named by Rotha, including the International League of Youth, the World Federation of Young Theosophists, the Order of the Round Table and the Star in the East Children's Clubs, all of which have internationalism at the heart of their message. She claimed that the Fascist Children's Clubs had been formed to counteract the spread of those doctrines 'until the Reds are turned out of the country'. There are definite echoes of the protectionism that would garner later support among the working classes.

The Women's Unit also fulfilled a role within the overall function of ensuring that Conservative public meetings proceeded without hindrance or interruption. While the BF membership could generally undertake this task, the presence of women adversaries at meetings proved difficult for male stewards to handle. The solution was to provide special women's units to remove female opponents from public meetings, but the women's units also strayed into disrupting left wing meetings on their own volition. Such activity became an integral part of being a member of the BF.

> In Birmingham the 1925 programme of events included infantry drill, a lecture on ju jitsu, a talk on how to tend injuries in a street accident or riot.[3]

Rotha's influence extended to the instigation of a Women's Fascist camp, perhaps harping back to her pre-war days with the Girl Guides, where the membership was introduced to the hardship and routine of living under canvas, and the discipline required to run an orderly camp. It would appear that the Women's Fascist camp came under attack from communists, perhaps a desirable turn of events from a training and toughening up point of view. The outcome was certainly that the women's spirits were sufficient to organise more such camps in following years.

Although Dorothy Dawney was an early member, if not founding member, of the BF, she was a little reluctant to show her true colours at this very early stage. Such reluctance may be attributed to her father-in-law's disapproval that his daughter-in-law should, in any way be involved with any political party except the old traditional Conservative Party; certainly not entering a political fight, of which he was critical of the present leadership. Once the old man was dead, then the change became really noticeable and her actions more extreme.

John and Dorothy Dawney were raised to the peerage in 1924, upon the death of John Dawney's father. Dorothy Dawney, now Viscountess Downe, did not begin to take a more active role in BF affairs until the General Strike of 1926, when she embarked on a series of public engagements, always promoting her fascist links and expressing her support for that organisation. Throughout her years as a member of the BF, she also served in the Conservative Party in various roles, and saw no conflict of interest.

Her first significant mention in the press as a fascist came on 20th March 1926 when she opened the Yorkshire headquarters of the BF in Leeds, claiming 500 local members. Interestingly, the opening ceremony was marked by the patriotic gesture of adding a final touch to a painting of the Union Flag on one of the walls. Always looking to make the right type of gesture on the social front, she also announced that the members had formed a panel who were prepared to be blood donors.[4]

Dorothy was also present when celebrity speakers visited Yorkshire, one such being Oliver Stillingfleet Locker-Lampson, member of Parliament for Birmingham Handsworth, also expressing concern about covert Bolshevik influence in Britain. He organised a number of public meetings under the title 'Clear out the Reds' and relied upon Rotha Lintorn-Orman's shock troops to provide security. A meeting in North Yorkshire was one such that went under the guise of an organised whist drive and dance organised by BF in Scarborough.

> He remembered when in Petrograd seeing a man speaking with a strange face - half Shakespeare and half Bernard Shaw, but with Hell in his eyes. The man preached death and destruction for the allied cause, faith and honour. It was Lenin. . . Among those present Viscountess Downe, County Commander of the Women's Units . . . Miss Lintorn Orman, founder of the British Fascists . . . there were about 300 present.[5]

At some meetings Dorothy was the main speaker, emphasizing that ethos of fascism as she saw it; putting the country first, upholding Christianity and encouraging individual effort. More significantly, asserting that there was no call for violence, unless the Government was not strong enough to deal effectively with the situation. According to the speakers who shared the platforms with her, violence was not on the BF agenda, but their support was available to the British Government should they weaken in the face of communism. The 'Red Flag' was anti-British and it was not going to be allowed to fly in London.

Dorothy, when she spoke at meetings, often pursued the topic dear to the heart of Rotha Lintorn-Orman, that of the influence of the communists on children, and she re-stated how the fascist movement should emulate the Scout and Guide movements of Rotha's youth, something which elements within the movement had criticised. Indeed much of the criticism from within the movement came from those who did not believe that Rotha was fascist enough. One such speech was reported in a local Yorkshire newspaper:

> One of the chief things that women were trying to do was to keep children from the influence of the Communists. She believed that in Hull there was at least one Communist Sunday school. These schools were difficult to trace, and the women's organisation tried to find out where their work was carried on. The idea of the Fascists was a perfect State in which men and women worked together for the good of the whole. They wanted this movement to be a kind of extension of the Boy Scout movement.[6]

The BF were fully aware of Dorothy's social position, and were quite prepared to exploit it to the full, with the grand setting of Wykeham Abbey, holding picnics, tea parties and the like in the splendid gardens. The early forms of the fascist movement were all but indistinguishable from the traditional Conservative Party, exploiting the natural advantages that breeding had provided. Location and surroundings were as important in persuading opponents to support a cause as ever.

In the main, members of BF were drawn from the minor gentry, and a little gracious living could provide a useful incentive to the most reluctant voter over to your point of view. There are some who might believe that the BF used the likes of Dorothy, Viscountess Downe, while excluding her from having a seat at the top table. Like most movements of the time, while women were in theory given equal rights to those of men, they were actually demoted to the role of 'assistants' in the real world. In this respect Rotha was something of an exception, but held her position of power only because she, through her mother, had hold of the purse strings.

We see here a fundamental difference between the BF and all the other forms of fascism - that is the failure to be based upon a 'Saviour' figure such as Mussolini in Italy, Hitler in Germany or even Moseley in later years as Britain approached another war. A basic premise of fascism, as was later defined, was that it demanded a charismatic leader around whom the rank and file could rally; a leader who could command loyalty and obedience, a leader who was feared by his or her followers.

> . . . a cult of the leader who promises national restoration in the face of humiliation brought on by supposed communists, Marxists and minorities and immigrants who are supposedly posing a threat to the character

> and the history of a nation . . . The leader proposes that only he can solve it and all of his political opponents are enemies or traitors.[7]

The above could be said to encompass Mussolini and Hitler certainly, Franco to a much lesser extent, and Moseley not at all. The BF, and Rotha Lintorn-Orman, fell well outside that description of fascism, instead wanting to preserve rather than supersede the established order. The BF had no easily identified opponent in their fight, just a nebulous notion of what they feared would happen should the existing system be cast aside in favour of socialism.

*Chapter 13*

# The General Strike

The origins of the discontent which was at the heart of the 1926 National Strike can be traced back into the war years, but the immediate provocation might be attributed just to the events that occurred on and around 'Black Friday', mentioned previously which, in 1921, imposed wage cuts upon the coal miners. Britain's coal exports had been significantly restricted during the war years, allowing other countries, particularly the United States, to expand their own coal industries. British coal output had reduced by a third since pre-war times.

The requirement for Germany to make reparation under the terms of the Treaty of Versailles was severely restricted by deflated world commodity prices which, in turn, prevented Germany earning sufficient foreign currency to fulfil its obligations to France and Italy and some other allied countries. In November 1922 Germany actually defaulted, provoking military action from France and Belgium, which in turn resulted in non-cooperation from German workers in factories that were under foreign occupation. France and Belgium had sent troops into Germany's main industrial area, the Ruhr Valley, with the aim of confiscating industrial goods as reparations payments. The German government ordered workers to follow a policy of 'passive resistance' i.e., to refuse to work or co-operate with the foreign troops, but in return the German government continued to pay their wages.

Coming three years after 'Black Friday', the Dawes Plan provided that Germany might export coal directly to France and Belgium as part of its reparations for the war, rather than sell their coal on the open market in order to raise funds with which to make reparations. This meant that payments in kind could be made without the world commodity price being a barrier in an already depressed market. A year later the British Government re-established the alignment of sterling to the price of gold thus, in turn, making exports more expensive for British producers and manufacturers, particularly the coal producers.

The 1924 General Election saw Winston Churchill appointed as Chancellor of the Exchequer in the Baldwin government. One of his first acts was to restore sterling to its pre First World War value against gold (gold standard), a decision welcomed by the Bank of England and the Conservative Party generally. Economists had fears about the move claiming potential damage to British exports, with coal a likely sufferer. Britain was not alone in taking this step, in 1922 all nations attending the Genoa Conference had agreed upon their aim of returning to the gold standard, some already had. More would at a future point.

Returning to the matter of war reparation, the Dawes Plan was developed by Charles Dawes, an American, who acted on behalf of the Reparations Commission, which had been established as a consequence of the Treaty of Versailles of 1919. The Plan was an attempt to end the French occupation of the Ruhr, which it had done in response to the German delay in fulfilling its obligations under the reparation programme. The acceptance of the Dawes Plan was not universal, neither within Germany nor amongst the Allies, but it was effective in ending the occupation and also overcame fears that a defeated Germany might be consumed by a military or political coup.

With the Dawes Plan in place, financial pressure on the British mining companies increased and they announced that there would be a further cut in coal miner's wages, and a new contract that extended the working day. This was directly in the face of the miners' slogan 'not a penny off the pay, not a minute on the day'. The Miners' Federation of Great Britain, the mine workers union, looked to the Trades Union Congress (TUC) for support, which in turn threatened industrial action by other trades unions, not directly involved, in support of the miners should the proposed cuts go ahead. Considering the outcome on 'Black Friday', the mine owners felt confident of the decision.

The strike had the TUC's support but it was no foregone conclusion that the strike would take place. They formed a negotiating committee which dealt directly with the Royal Commission on the Coal Industry, led by Sir Herbert Samuel and better known as the Samuel Commission, during which time TUC made many counter proposals to the government's plan to reduce wages. The main problem was that the TUC were in a negotiating role rather than a decision making role, and that it was the individual unions that held the whip hand at every stage.

The threat of a General Strike had seemed very real at the end of July 1925 and this had prompted the formation of a right wing volunteer organisation to take over the jobs of striking workers, should such an emergency arise. The formation of this volunteer organisation was largely down to the initiative of Rotha Lintorn-Orman and the BF who went to the Government with their proposal for an Organisation for the Maintenance of Supplies (OMS) which they believed would counteract the effects of the impending Socialist threat.

The strategy was accepted, but instead of allowing the BF to continue, in September 1925 the OMS was taken under the wing of the Government, in the form of a managing committee to be chaired by Lord Hardinge, who in turn stipulated that the organisation must be non-political. Specifically, it was decided that the BF should not be included in the scheme unless it removed the word 'Fascist' from its name and that it would also have to abandon its own management structure, submitting to the dictates of the committee.

The impending General Strike, due to begin on 4 May 1926, was the start of the gradual splitting up of the BF and was the catalyst that gave rise to more extreme organisations which then culminated in the rise of Oswald Mosley and the British Union of Fascists (BUF). The fact that the General Strike was fairly peaceful, and that it did not result in a left wing coup, took some urgency away from the popular fear of the long term threat to the British way of life and to the British Empire.

> An exercise in moderation and constraint, the nine-day strike cruelly exposed the lack of factual substance at the heart of the BF's alarmist anti-labour rhetoric. With the failure of the General Strike and the waning of trade union militancy in its aftermath, there appeared little

> justification for a paramilitary civil defence force. These developments would effectively deprive the BF of a core element in its ideology, resulting in a loss of political direction.[1]

Rotha Lintorn-Orman was adamant that the BF would not compromise its independence by accepting the authority of the committee. Having taken this view, she was in immediate conflict with Viscountess Downe and with General Blakeney, both of whom were prepared to join the OMS under the terms that the committee dictated. The Fascist Grand Council came down on the side of Rotha, who held the purse strings, and by doing so forced Blakeney's resignation.

However the BF maintained transport units and provided an organisational structure for the OMS while not being actual members. Questions were raised in parliament as to the legality of this situation but members were reminded that the OMS, while remaining a volunteer organisation, was free to operate according to its own rules as long as they remained within the law – even communists.

Lord Hardinge's committee, which led the OMS, was not without its critics. Those on the left, felt it hid beneath the cloak of fascism and likened it to the American Ku Klux Klan and the Italian Blackshirts. The Metropolitan Police had such misgivings that its Commissioner refused to co-operate with it, although police forces in other parts of the country thought differently.

In reality neither the OMS nor the BF were much used during the General Strike, nor were a number of other right wing groups who offered their services. The government found that those on strike caused fewer problems than had been feared, there was a need to make up for missing services, but the maintenance of law and order was well within the means of each and every local police force.

Blakeney, along with Rear Admiral A. E. Armstrong who was both his friend and supporter, formed another group which they called The Loyalists, which was immediately accepted into the OMS, providing them some degree of validity. Viscountess Downe did not follow their lead but stayed with Rotha and the BF. Two other leading members did follow Blakeney into the British Loyalists, Patrick Boyle the Earl of Glasgow and Lord Ernest Hamilton, all three later joined Arnold Leese in the National Fascists.

Boyle held extremist views and played an active role in a number of right wing groups and claimed to have seen, first hand, Bolshevik terror groups at work. Hamilton was a Conservative politician sitting for an Irish seat. He was a novelist of some note but also penned a number of historical works based upon the connection between Ulster and the Scottish borders. He held Christian views which were, to say the least, somewhat highly anti-Semitic in nature.

With Blakeney and his supporters gone, Rotha stepped forward to regain some of the influence lost to those of a more pragmatic disposition. She decided, with or without the approval of the committee, that she would deploy her followers to help combat the effects of the impending socialist inspired disruption. The solution would be the formation of the Q Divisions, drawn from the remaining female membership, and taking on the same tasks as the OMS approved groups, but under her personal command.

The Q Divisions were a band of young women who were chosen from amongst the membership of the BF to become shock troops, at Rotha's personal command, and who would relish the opportunity to join a 'rough house'. These were the young women invited down to Over Langford Manor for robust games and training. In London, the Q Divisions were transported from event to event in open backed lorries, ostensibly to steward meetings, but more often than not to cause disruption.

The Q Divisions were also employed, during the General Strike, to provide protection for those speaking and protesting against the strikers. There were instances reported of politicians, feeling unable to venture into certain industrial areas, being accompanied by Q Division squads to ensure their safety. The over enthusiasm of Rotha's supporters often led to conflict, not only with the Socialists but also with the police called upon to re-establish law and order. The confrontational and militaristic leanings of Rotha were well suited to the conflict ahead, but physical measures were not confined to one side only.

> A wickedly provocative circular by the National Fascists, accusing the General Strike leaders of being enemy agents in foreign pay and calling for volunteers to help blackleg, roused fury among the workers of Hammersmith. A large body of police were necessary to keep them from storming the Fascist headquarters. The conflict lasted for hours and many arrests were made.[2]

There was a continuous war by pamphlet on both sides. From the unions their successful actions in multiple local theatres of conflict were lauded, as were numerous indications of support from socialist organisations across the world; the very 'internationalism' that the fascists feared. The voice of the Government, combatting the General Strike, was the *British Gazette* where it was reported that fascists, not adverse to confrontation, were being paid to distribute it on the streets.

The strike began on 5 May and the first few days were largely uneventful, but on 8 May the Government employed the Army to protect lorries carrying food out of London Docks; on Baldwin's insistence, the soldiers were unarmed. Pickets had been successful in imposing a stranglehold on the docks and London had little more than two days supply of flour and bread, but having broken the picket line, there was little or no violence shown by those on strike.

Elsewhere in the country public transport manned by workers breaking the strike were attacked, with considerable damage to vehicles, most notably to the *Flying Scotsman* being derailed north of Newcastle with over 500 passengers on board. This pattern was replayed throughout the country with the more serious actions being witnessed in remote cities and towns, but the focal points being attributed to London as the seat of power and therefore more noteworthy.

The ending of the General Strike on 12 May signalled the end of the Trades Union Congress organised industrial action. This followed a ruling by the High Court that the industrial action within the coal industry was legitimate, but the dispute between the Trades Union Congress and the Government was not a trades dispute as such, and thus did not fall within the protection of the Trades Disputes Act of 1906. The result could mean the sequestration of the Trades Union Congress funds, and also those of other individual trades unions.

Keith Layboun in his book *The General Strike, Day by Day* sums up the General Strike in the following way:

> In the final analysis, the General Strike revealed the real weakness of a constitutional trade union movement supporting a course of action to which it was reluctantly committed and whose consequences would have to be measured in political as well as industrial terms. In effect the General Council, doubting its own ability to sustain the General Strike, convinced itself of the need for industrial peace and forced a resolute government to do little other than attempt to maintain the movement of vital food supplies until the conflict was called off. The General Strike was therefore a landmark in British history, for it revealed to the General Council the limits of its own industrial policy in the face of a powerful and committed government.[3]

The declaration that the General Strike was over only slowly brought the country back to normal. Not all industrial action ended suddenly on 12 May; many did not return to work for some time after, despite the risk of litigation. The miners, of course, continued but were finally forced to return to work towards the end of the year, with reduced wages and longer hours, the miners having to negotiate with individual mine owners, rather than nationally through the Miners' Federation of Great Britain.

Rotha, in the euphoria of victory, organised a rally for both men and women members in Hyde Park on Sunday, 6 June. This included not only London detachments but also those from Southampton, Hampshire, Birmingham and other provincial centres, numbering about 1,000 in all. There was some heckling but it remained peaceful despite some in the crowd forcing their way to the platform, only to be ejected. The delegates also gathered at the Cenotaph, where Rotha laid a black and white wreath, a replica of the British Fascists' badge.

Rotha's part in the breaking of the General Strike, and the employment of her 'Q' Divisions in London, is not given great prominence in relating the events of the strike but is often lost in tales of the 'volunteers' who manned the buses, delivered milk, worked the signal boxes etc. Her role was better known at the time, and at that time she and her all female group were seen as a modern phenomenon.

In November of 1926 the *Daily News* carried an interview with Rotha under the headline 'The Fascist Amazons' in which there is a rare insight of her character and personality, if the newspaper report can be believed.

> Who are the women, enrolled in a special patrol of the British Fascists, whose main hobby in life is hurling women interrupters, Communists preferred, out of 'patriotic' meetings? . . . Their latest exploit was at a meeting of the Imperial League at Kentish Town Baths, when 15 women hecklers (in the words of the Chief of

> the Patrol) [were] slung bodily out of the building on to the pavement . . . sought out Miss Lintorn-Orman, who is described as their Chief of Staff.
>
> I found myself gazed upon by eyes the colour of tempered steel . . . in a voice as cold as a December morning, 'Precisely what was my business?' . . . She pressed a button, a bell rang, and the door opened to admit a uniformed figure dressed severely in black and – like the Chief herself – shingled.[4] Advancing the regulation number of paces, the subordinate brought her heels together with a resounding click and stood rigidly to attention.
>
> Casualties so far as this troop of Amazons who, I was told, have been selected out of 1,000 women for their courage, loyalty and 'usefulness' have been bruised shins only. 'They are expert wrestlers, good at ju-jitsu, and have never been known to lose their heads in a crisis. . . And if ever we meet men Communists masquerading as women, and interfering with us, we shall really go for them.
>
> 'Good-bye', and with the most disarming of smiles she dismissed me.[5]

While Rotha was engaged with the affairs of the management of the BF, her mother Blanch was still actively engaged with public meetings, despite women speakers being roughly handled. At the beginning of each meeting Blanch, or another, would make a public declaration that they would hold the meeting 'at all costs', a declaration that would be backed up by a number of male stewards, plus some tough women stewards to handle the ladies.

There is very little that gives a real insight into Rotha's character; the interview above gives a rare view of the Rotha that was known to her friends and colleagues, although in fairness it may be one distorted by the individual prejudices of that particular newspaperman. It should not be forgotten that the above report concentrates on the strangeness of the scene, and the masculinity of the BF women, than of the message that they profess.

## *Chapter 14*

# Fault Lines

Although the anti-socialist lobby had gained the day, and Rotha and the BF could congratulate themselves on a victory, the end of the General Strike left them with a marked difficulty. On the one hand the communist threat was seen to have passed, and thus reduced the seriousness and urgency of the fascist message; on the other hand the need for a uniformed military style counter-force was shown to have little foundation in reality, the strike having been defeated in the courts. It was time for the BF to re-group and reconsider the next move.

Rotha was again in control of the BF, and so Over Langford Manor in Somerset beckoned to her as a retreat from the intense political life in the metropolis. The internal wrangling with Blakeney, Leese and others, the disputes with Lord Hardinge and the OMS, and the physical confrontations with those on strike had taken its toll on a battle weary young woman. Not only that, but she was fighting a war of attrition, as a woman, trying to keep control of a political party that had seen defeat while bathing in the spoils of success.

Rotha appears to have put frenetic political activity on the back burner for a while and concentrated on rekindling her previous emphasis on a militaristic, almost Spartan, group of young women who could operate as her shock troops if the need arose again. The effectiveness of her 'Q' Division troops had demonstrated their worth during the brief General Strike, and she and the BF would be available to aid the British monarchy, whether or not the British Government called for their help. More importantly they would be in a position to come to the aid of the monarch against a socialist government if the British government failed in its duty.

Her early years in the Girl Guides, with its uniform, discipline and outdoor life, was still exercising a great control on her thinking and Blakeney's likening the BF to an adult version of the Boy Scouts was proving to be quite valid. Her war years, spent with a group of very masculine women drivers, had a very definite influence on her – not to undervalue in any way the bravery she had shown in that theatre of war. She now sought out the camaraderie of the women who formed the 'Q' Divisions, perhaps as a patrol leader might take her patrol camping.

The best insight we might gain on everyday life at Over Langford Manor can be found in a memoire written by Francis Wookey in 2003. Wookey was born and grew up at Myrtle Cottage, about a hundred yards from the Manor House, where his father worked from about 1921. When Rotha was away from Over Langford Manor on BF business, Francis Wookey's parents acted as housekeepers. During those years, the young Francis and his brother Arthur spent quite a lot of time at the Manor and, according to his memoire, were left with many happy memories of those days.

His recollection of Rotha's appearance echoes others, and completely matches the impression given by photographs of her, both as an ambulance driver during the war and as the leader of the BF at the time of the General Strike.

> My early recollection of Miss Orman was of a tall, gaunt masculine female – always dressed in an open necked shirt and corduroy breeches, thick long wollen stockings and heavy brown brogue shoes. While at her Langford base she would partake in any job on the farm that was being performed – mucking out the cows and pigs or hay making. She drove a high powered American built car – an Oakland – I never saw another of this make.[1]

The motorcar was most probably an Oakland Six, which was the first six-cylinder engine car built by the Oakland Motor Company, a division of Michigan based General Motors, and was a very impressive piece of machinery. In terms of image, it suited Rotha's character perfectly; strong and powerful, with an awe inspiring presence, and not able to be easily ignored or overlooked. The Oakland Six personified the image of the Chicago Mafia, an image appropriate to the tactics of the BF, and one that Rotha sought to exploit.

The motorcar that Rotha chose as her personal form of transport was entirely in keeping with what we know of her character. She attempted to surround herself with the trappings of power, real or imaginary, and saw herself as a force to be reckoned with. This can be seen in the manner in which she presents herself to the newspaper reporter that interviewed her, surrounded by tough looking women she projected an aura of menace. Her entire life, including perhapsher setting up of the

BF, was under the control of her mother. It's interesting that this alter ego might be an attempt for Rotha to isolate herself from Blanch; or to live up to her expectations.

Blanch seems to play little part in Rotha's day-to-day life, except to provide her with an out of town rural retreat. There is no suggestion that Rotha's family was any part of her life; there are no records that indicate any interaction with any other person at an intimate level at all. It would not be unreasonable to describe Rotha as being insular in nature. With the exception of Nesta Maude, in the years they spent at Forest Mere, she seems not to have forged any friendships from a mass of acquaintances.

She must have cut a striking figure in rural Somerset, a tall girl striding about the farm with the confidence that comes from having seen active service and having a troop of like young women at her beck and call. When in London she was in constant conflict, even in danger from some of her opponents. In the wilds of Somerset, she could have a little time for herself and away from her mother. Here she was free to enjoy her unconventional lifestyle away from the glare of publicity.

In the seclusion of her Somerset retreat, Rotha was able to invite likeminded young women to spend time with her for 'training' weekends, where they could indulge in games and physical exercises. Given the rumours circulating at the time, and the physical nature of the training, it seems very likely that the 'games' involved a significant degree of physical contact. These gatherings were residential and it is difficult to believe that they did not include some degree of sexual activity.

> Obviously her tough wartime role was responsible for her entry in to the Fascist movement – or prime founder – this was before the rise of Oswald Mosley. I can well remember the Swastika flag flying from the flagpole on the lawn of the Manor. Quite a number of her fellow fascist hardline female members would congregate at the Manor from time to time – they would take part in rough sporting activities in the field next to the Manor.[2]

The period of reflection that followed the General Strike allowed Rotha time to find new justification for the BF's militarised, rather than political, approach. Recent experience had taught them that the Government had usurped their position of readiness by the creation of, or the taking over of, the OMS. Should a similar situation arise in the future, Rotha determined that instead of there being an unorganised and disparate group of organisations flocking to support the Government, the BF would already be in place as a force to be reckoned with.

One of the cornerstones of the BF was its loyalty to the monarch, as well as to the country and Empire, with a rather distorted notion of exactly where the monarch sat within the British constitutional structure. With this in mind Rotha sought support for her group from those close to the Royal Family and members such as Viscountess Dorothy Downe, lady-in-waiting to Queen Mary, were extremely valuable allies. There are accounts, already mentioned, of the BF marching to the Cenotaph to lay wreaths, and to St Paul's Cathedral for consecration of their colours. Rotha herself made application to use the Royal Crown on their publications, but was denied.

Rumours began to circulate, within the BF and among its detractors, about Rotha's sexual predilections and of her growing addiction to drugs. These were not necessarily accurate in every detail but were fundamentally true, more particularly they offered a weapon with which her detractors could undermine her, and through her the BF and her supporters. Most significantly, Blanch Lintorn-Orman, who was providing funds for Rotha and the BF to continue, was not impressed. Rotha's behaviour was causing concern and the more genteel among the upper classes were likely to fall by the wayside.

With Rotha was growing away from Blanch's control, it seems possible that Blanch may have used the most powerful weapon she possessed in order to re-establish some control over her daughter. There is no evidence that Rotha had an opportunity to establish any personal wealth in the years since 1923, and it is very clear that Blanch remained the source for the funding of the BF; any threat to remove that support would be a powerful card for Blanch to play. It would mean not only that Rotha would be financially vulnerable, but also the means by which the BF continued to operate would be at risk.

The nature of the rumours cannot be verified but are most likely to have involved her style of dress, her mannishness and her assumed debauched lifestyle. Over Langford Manor house offered the seclusion that she desired, while the company she kept there would have attracted much attention in the area. It seems quite feasible that her mother may have retained some old friendships within the Langford or Churchill area and that such contacts would have kept Blanch up-to-date with the goings on at the Manor House. Alcohol would have certainly featured, but whether Rotha was into drugs at this point is open to question.

Following the disagreements within the BF at the time of the General Strike, Rotha's split with Robert Blakeney was never to be healed, her disagreement with Viscountess Downe was not so fundamental that they were not soon reconciled. However, a new adversary was waiting unnoticed in the shadows when Oswald Mosley won the 1926 Smethwick by-election and took his seat in Parliament on the Labour benches. He had previously sat in Parliament as a Conservative, crossing the floor because of the Conservative policy in Ireland.

In 1927, Mosley described the British Fascists as 'black-shirted buffoons, making a cheap imitation of ice-cream sellers', no doubt reflecting Rotha's enthusiasm, or obsession, with Mussolini's version of fascism. A few years later, following a tour visiting various European fascist movements he returned with a much more approving view of Mussolini's plans, and thought 'national socialism' a much better model for Britain than 'international socialism'; the former being a model that Adolph Hitler in Germany was attempting to bring about.

In actual fact, despite the name, 'national socialism' was not what Hitler and his henchmen really had in mind for Germany's future. Instead of it following a socialist manifest it, instead, followed a dictatorial path which would eventually lead to a police state. One might argue that this was not so different from the Mussolini model, or even that which was proposed by Rotha's fascists with their very British take on fascism. This is why, when Mosley tried to force the German version of fascism upon the British, he found that his most significant opponent was Rotha Lintorn-Orman.

A more significant opponent of Rotha's in the late 1920s was the man who first defected from the BF during the lead up to the General Strike. This was Arnold Leese who went on to form the Imperial Fascist League in 1928. Leese was as equally convinced as Rotha for the need to command a uniformed force in order to counter the communist threat, and the formation of his black shirt paramilitary unit, with its very public persona, within the Imperial Fascist League placed her at a disadvantage in recruiting those willing to become shock troops.

> Leese had become so alienated that he seriously believed that the British aristocracy had been corrupted by Jews as a result of repeated marriages with wealthy Jewesses designed to restore the tottering finances of landed families. He also condemned the Church because he felt that it had become warped by dubious Judaic doctrines including pacifism, internationalism and the brotherhood of man.[3]

The Imperial Fascist League was much more anti-Semitic than was the BF, who simply saw the Jews as being in league with socialists and communists. Arnold Leese sought to remove the Jews from Britain, by force if necessary, and began to associate himself much more with Adolph Hitler and his brand of fascism. Rotha did not see herself at odds with the British Government, albeit a Labour government, and certainly not with the King and the British establishment. She sought to protect and maintain the status quo and protect it from those who would damage the country and the Empire, however misguided her actions.

> Leese despised American society because it included a large proportion of citizens of 'inferior racial stock' who caused crime and disorder and made politics even more degenerate than in Britain. But Britain, too, suffered excessive numbers of 'undesirables', that is naturalized aliens. Leese proposed to deal with them by drawing a distinction between 'British Citizens', who, alone, would be entitled to full rights such as voting and serving in governments, and 'British Subjects'; the first group would be confined to people of 'pure British blood or when of foreign origin . . . only white European races with a strong preference for the Nordic. A convinced eugenicist, Leese also aimed to increase the birth rate among the middle classes and to check procreation among the unfit which, he believed, went against the laws of nature.[4]

There was some confusion over the various fascist groups at the time. The Imperial Fascist League was a major player with many smaller and less significant groups seeking some sort of recognition. But in fact the only organisation of any significance was the Imperial Fascist League. Rotha was very quick in trying to separate herself from Leese's new organisation, and his stated claim to be the only organisation consecrated to the service of the British race and Empire.

> The British Fascists have been in existence since May 1923, and have always adhered to the original aim, namely, to be in a position to give every service to H.M. the King and to any loyal Government in power in the event of attempted revolution or general strike. The British Fascists are absolutely non-political.[5]

The closing of the second decade of the twentieth century also saw the beginnings of the Great Depression, hitting the working class population in the north the hardest. America was first to feel the effects of this world-wide crisis, but the plight of Britain was equally severe. Where America had experienced a post war boom, Britain had hardly recovered from the recent war. The Depression in Britain was not in such contrast to its immediate past as it was in America, although the consequences were equally dire.

The New York Stock Market crashed, and the reverberations were felt around the world. The effect on British manufacturing was devastating, with calls for nationalisation of key industries. With exports much in decline the protectionist policies, first called for by Rotha and the BF, were gaining a new foothold in the country. However, a far stronger force was in the wings, waiting for an opportunity to breathe the oxygen of unrest and develop into a dominant political, as well as a martial, power in the country. This was the result of the 'Mosley Memorandum', leading the way to the formation of the New Party which in turn led to the formation of the British Union of Fascists.

The Mosley Referendum largely echoed Rotha Lintorn-Orman's own calls for an end to internationalism and the imposition of higher tariffs on imported goods in order to give some protection to British industry and agriculture. It also called for a strengthening of the bonds within the British Empire and the development of trade within the Empire, to a level that it would constitute a self-reliant and self-sufficient autarky.

The worrying aspect of Mosley's thinking, which was never an aspect of Rotha's public statements, were the echoes of the path down which Adolf Hitler was travelling. Although Mosley saw fascism as ultimately coming to power via the ballot box, once elected, he believed that a fascist leader would naturally award himself, and a small group of acolytes and experts, executive powers superseding those of the elected representatives. Such a process was not dissimilar to the route that Mussolini had taken in Italy.

*Chapter 15*

# From Old to New

Following the General Strike and its 'damp squib' conclusion, Rotha Lintorn-Orman turned her attention to Northern Ireland, sometimes incorrectly referred to as Ulster,[1] and the loyalist support that might be fostered there. There were hopes, unfulfilled in fact, that a resurgent group in the Irish Free State would grow to call for re-unification. In Northern Ireland plans were mooted to convert the failing BF into a group specifically to fight to reverse the separation of the two parts of the island of Ireland.

The situation for the BF worsened, membership continued to decline and Rotha lost support from both sides of her organisation. Her attempts to move away from the ultra-conservative line and adopt a more Italian style of fascism, with its increasing anti-Semitic emphasis, caused more division. Many began to favour the even more extreme brand of fascism found in Germany; others, including Viscountess Downe, sought to remain within the Conservative Party and promote loyalty to the monarch and to the Empire.

Rotha devoted much more of her time, and of her mother's wealth, to promoting the cause in Northern Ireland where there was a specific goal for her to achieve. Over time her health began to suffer and rumours again began to circulate about her eccentric behaviour and her relying more and more on alcohol, and possibly drugs. She was a heavy smoker and spent some part of each winter in Las Palmas on Gran Canaria soaking up the sun.

If she was taking drugs it was most probably one of the opiates, such as opium, morphine or cocaine, which were the drugs of choice for the wealthy during the late twenties. They were easy to obtain and, as well as being recreational, they would have offered some relief from any lingering effects of the malaria from which she suffered during the war years. The uncontrolled availability of drugs to soldiers and ex-soldiers after the war, when the medical profession was largely in control, had given way to controlled distribution after the passing of the Dangerous Drugs Acts of 1920 and 1923.

She made these visits to Las Palmas alone, not with Blanch, and this may have been an opportunity for Rotha to find a little private time away from her mother's influence. If the malaria virus was still in her body, then the warmth of the Canary Islands must have brought her some relief, and from the strain of the General Strike and the growing threat from Blakeney, Leese and now Moseley, on the rise. She may well have resorted to alcohol, even drugs, as a way of coping with the ongoing symptoms.

During her many visits to Northern Ireland she spoke repeatedly of the dangers she saw in the 'Red Sunday Schools' springing up all over the country, which was something that the BF would campaign to have closed. She spoke of loyalty to the King and country, rather than loyalty to any specific political party, and distanced the BF from the more militant fascist groups. She often complained of the apathy that was permitting the rise of Bolshevism over the maintenance of the British Empire in its then current form.

In her speeches, Rotha argued against 'internationalism' and urged financial support for British manufactured items and agricultural produce. Her message began to lean ever further toward the concept of removing foreigners from the country in order to provide jobs for British workers, and investment by and for British industry. Her figure of a quarter of a million aliens entering Britain each year was rarely challenged at these meetings.

Rotha did not abandon efforts to keep the BF to the fore in mainland Britain, specifically by policing meetings with her all women special patrols, working in conjunction with the men's units. Such outings for the women's special patrols were not confined to the cities. Provincial towns, especially in the surroundings of Langford, where Rotha's summer camps were held, were the scenes of much smaller, open-air meetings.

Whereas the rural meetings tended to be small and uneventful, those in the city, especially in London, were somewhat confrontational. Reading accounts of some meetings it seems that it was Rotha and the BFs that went looking for trouble, rather than being the innocent victims, needing to defend themselves.

> In response to a challenge, the British Fascists . . . held a meeting at the Poplar Town Hall. Remembering their experiences at Canning Town, where their women were roughly handled the Fascists brought a great body of 'Stewards'. . . Lintorn-Orman's declaration . . . hold the meeting at all costs . . . one man tried to get on the platform to speak, but he was promptly 'tackled' by a watchful steward . . . women looked smart in their

> uniforms of black coat, grey skirt, grey felt hat, grey tie, grey stockings and black shoes . . . At the close they formed up outside the Town Hall under police protection and the care of their 'stewards' and marched back to Aldgate, police on either side, and a lorry full of more stewards safeguarding the rear.[2]

With the British Union of Fascists making their presence more pronounced on the streets, open battles were seen on the streets of London between the various women's contingents. One all-out battle was reported in which Mosley's blackshirts raided a Lintorn-Orman's blueshirt meeting with the intention of breaking it up, only to encounter a third group, the Imperial Fascist League headed by Arnold Leese, wearing a less marked form of dress.

A year later, two of Hitler's brownshirts, in full Storm Trooper uniform, paid an unannounced visit to the BF headquarters in Stanhope Gardens, only to be immediately recalled to Germany in deep trouble with Berlin. This seems to have been an error on the part of the two Storm Troopers, either through engaging with the wrong fascist group, or misunderstanding Germany's policy regarding exporting the Nazi version of fascism.

At this point the BF began to leach members to other, more extreme, fascist parties. Rotha had never really embraced the version of fascism which so many had found to be their chosen version, such as the anti-Semitic views of Arnold Leese, and this was the trait that was becoming more prevalent amongst the entire community of fascist supporters.

This was also the point at which her dependence upon alcohol, and perhaps drugs, became problematical for both Rotha and for the BFs. It's not clear whether withdrawing of funds was an attempt by Blanch to curb Rotha's excessive lifestyle or whether she was truly running out of money. What we don't know, and may never know, is the extent to which Rotha's dependence on alcohol was an attempt by her to counteract the effects of illness contracted in Serbia; either way, Rotha made her annual trip to Las Palmas again, perhaps to think things through.

Rotha Lintorn-Orman sailed on the TMS *Apapa*, of the Elder Dempster Line, departing 6 February 1935 from Liverpool, and bound for Las Palmas, although West Africa was the final destination for most of those on board. She gave her residence as 68 Longridge Road in Earls Court but offered no occupation. Interestingly, despite her wealth she was travelling second class and, according to the passenger list, was planning to return to England rather than stay on the island.

A few weeks later Rotha was in the village of Santa Brígida, not far from Las Palmas, as had become her routine in recent winters. With her health failing from the illness and disease that she had experienced in Serbia, made worse from her continued abuse of alcohol and drugs, the cold weather she left behind at home had caused additional problems for her. Of course she smoked heavily, and the damp British winters did not help her condition.

On 10 March she finally succumbed to her condition and died. She was buried in the English Cemetery at Las Palmas, an Anglican cemetery in a Catholic country. Although originally restricted to British nationals, since 1875 it had become the final resting place for Anglicans from many other countries. Gran Canaria was a port of call for travellers between Britain and Africa and had developed into a very cosmopolitan island with a protestant church completed before the turn of the century.

Her gravestone bears an inscription for Rotha Berly Lintorn Lintorn-Orman, the misspelling of Beryl perhaps emphasising her isolation from fellow countrymen and family in that remote outpost. There were limited references to her death, except in the Irish press.

> Miss R. L. Lintorn-Orman, a great friend of Ulster, passed away at Las Palmas on March 10, 1935. Daughter of the late Major Charles Orman and granddaughter of the late Field-Marshal Sir Lintorn Simmons, she worked during the war for the women's reserve ambulance, the Scottish Women's Hospital Corps, with which she sailed for active service in Siberia in 1916. She served on the Drina Front as an ambulance driver, and was awarded the Croix de Charitie (twice) for gallantry. In 1917, on being invalided home, she joined the British Red Cross Society, and was appointed commandant in charge of the motor school at Devonshire House, where she won golden opinions for her efficiency. To fight Communism, she founded in May 1923, the organisation known as British Fascists, and during the General Strike in 1926 members could not be enrolled quickly enough. Miss Lintorn-Orman was an ardent Loyalist, and, connected with the Loyal Orange Order in Ulster, spoke at the

> July celebrations in 1930. A memorial service in tribute to her was held at St. Giles-in-the-Fields, London, on April 7th.[3]

Four months later, in July 1935, the BF ceased to exist. The company bearing that name, which had been the vehicle through which the movement was governed, was wound-up by the Official Receiver at a meeting of creditors and shareholders. It seems the company's books were 'kept in a lax, casual manner' and there was evidence that records of meetings suggested that there had been 'continual dissention' between members of the governing councils. Lack of income had been the catalyst for failure, income having dwindled to a few hundred pounds per year, and the foreclosure on a guaranteed loan had forced the winding-up petition.

After Rotha's death, Blanch Lintorn-Orman remained at 68 Longridge Road in Earls Court, sharing with three other people. By 1939, according to the England and Wales Register, she was living out of London at Lynwood House in Church Avenue, Farnborough. With her, at that address, were Alma Wroughton, Fredrick Moffitt, Yvonne Thomson, and Angela Woods, a young actress and singer. Blanch died 30 November 1941, leaving £22,355 including the Langford estate, but leaving a lifetime tenancy to Averil Colby at the property in Somerset.

Why Averil Colby should have had the benefit of a lifetime tenancy of the Upper Langford estate is not clear but a 1926 newspaper identifies her as being the secretary of the Somerset branch of the BF, although there are few references beyond the

Francis Wookey memoire, referred to earlier, in which he also mentions a Miss Wilkinson.

During the nineteen twenties and thirties Averil was living on the Over Langford estate and ran the dairy smallholding which also produced butter and cheese. Daughter of a doctor, she came originally from Yorkshire and joined Rotha at Over Langford after leaving Studley Agricultural College in Warwickshire but with Rotha's drug and alcohol abuse, disagreement was inevitable and she left to live with her widowed mother, first in Devon and then in Hampshire, before finally returning to Upper Langford after Rotha's death.

Although the BF were now quite defunct, there was a hiatus within the spectrum of the general fascist movement. Even though Rotha's group had not proven up to the task of establishing fascism as the basis for a political movement of any substance, its longevity and its origins from within the suffrage movement had given it a more positive credential, through its love of King and country, than the growing negative hatred and anti-Semitism being offered by others.

Oswald Mosley's New Party was the most significant of the myriad of fascist parties that sought to take the place once held by Rotha and the BF, albeit following the German rather than the Italian model. Other embryonic fascist parties, begun in the late 1920s or early 30s, included the Imperial Fascist League under Arnold Leese, the Scottish Democratic Fascist Party formed by the Scottish members of the New Party and the short lived British United Fascists. Most of those fascist organisations, contemporary with the New Party, or its successor, were beaten back either by subscription income, or by physical bullying.

The New Party had been formed in early 1931 by Oswald Mosley after his second Mosley Memorandum was rejected by the Labour Party, for whom he was now a sitting Member of Parliament, having 'crossed the floor' once before in 1920. At the 1931 General Election the New Party put forward twenty-four candidates, but achieved no victory. Its best success was with Sellick Davies in Merthyr Tydfil and Oswald Mosley himself in Stoke on Trent, polling 30 per cent and 24 per cent respectively, achieving 2nd and 3rd places in the poll. The New Party's entry into the election took votes from Labour rather than from the Conservatives, the New Party being perceived as a socialist schism.

Both Mosley and his wife Cynthia Curzon were Labour members of Parliament, he for Smethwick and she for Stoke on Trent, but it was Mosley rather than Cynthia that fought the Stoke on Trent seat at the 1931 election. Cynthia, before her resignation from Labour and her joining the *New Party*, had led an unsuccessful campaign for Britain to offer Leon Trotsky political asylum. Lord and Lady Mosley presented an unlikely image of a committed socialist couple steeped in the ethos of the left.

Cynthia's death in 1933 allowed Oswald Mosley to resume the bachelor life that he had known prior to his marriage in 1920, although he was known to have had affairs with his wife's younger sister, and their father's second wife, before Cynthia's death. Mosley also had an affair with Diana Guinness who was married to Bryan Guinness, heir to the Irish brewing dynasty. Bryan and Diana Guinness were divorced in 1932, and she and Mosley were then married in 1936, with the consequence that the eccentric Mitford family, in the form of Diana Mitford, entered the political arena.

Mosley's growing interests in the Italian and German fascist movements was mirrored by those of Diana who had visited Germany, and attended both Nuremberg rallies as a guest of Adolph Hitler, her sister Unity being on quite friendly terms with him. In 1936 Diana returned to Germany for the Berlin Olympic games as Hitler's guest. There she spent time with Joseph and Magda Goebbels, returning later that same year when she and Oswald Mosley were married in the Goebbels home, with Adolph Hitler as one of the guests.

> At the wedding breakfast, a luncheon for twelve at the Goebbels' villa at Wannsee, with a special vegetarian dish for Hitler, Diana regaled her host with a blow-by-blow account of a scandal still known only to a small circle: the new King of England was obsessively in love with the American Wallis Simpson, who was about to divorce her second husband.[4]

On Mosley's instructions, the marriage was to kept secret. No photographs were taken through fear of them reaching the British press. Mr and Mrs Mosley returned to Britain with only Diana's sister Unity knowing their secret. Diana, however, did tell the Mitford family, but they managed to contain the story within the family and a close circle of intimates.

*Chapter 16*

# Conclusion

Any assessment of the life of Rotha Lintorn-Orman must be based solely on the events of her life reported by others, as she herself penned very little and nothing at all about her thoughts or feelings. Her childhood is only recorded by chance, in that her youthful companion wrote about her own childhood, but included no sign of her own or Rotha's inner thoughts. Her war years were eventful, hidden behind organisational detail while serving in London, but she was not specifically named in any memoirs covering her time in Serbia or Greece despite receiving awards for her service.

Her political life was not one in which she sought personal fame, but confined her actions to supporting her vision, even being prepared to give up some control to others in order to advance that cause, and prepared to dig her heels in should others try to take her campaign in a different direction. It would be reasonable to suggest that she was not anti-Semitic, not that she didn't blame the Jewish financiers for many of the ills of the world, but there is no evidence to suggest she held any animosity towards the Jews as a race.

Her death was, to say the least, ignominious. Alone in death, not in her own country, and to a great extent abandoned by those she held close. She was riddled with alcohol and drugs, perhaps by choice, perhaps driven by her wartime experiences.

She was buried in a graveyard on the outskirts of Las Palmas which has since fallen into disuse and dereliction. Her grave is still marked, but with only the stray cats of Gran Canaria to visit, and even her headstone contains errors of fact.

She died, as she was born, into a nuclear family, with no close friends in evidence. Both her parents came from military backgrounds; on her mother's side from the upper echelons of society, on her father's side from the more down to earth British in India. Her playfellows were royalty and their court followers drawn from her mother's friends, rather than those of her father; indeed there appears to be little or no contact with the father's family at all, despite them being more numerous than those of her mother.

She seems to have been under the influence of her mother to some extent during her long childhood, understandably so in the early years, but with no sign of rebellion as adolescence dawned. It's interesting that a companion was found for Rotha as this stage approached, chosen at random it appeared, but nevertheless 'suitable' in every aspect. Nesta not only fulfilled that role but also that of friend, travelling companion, sharer of hobbies – but not that of confidante. In her entire autobiography, Nesta did not mention what she or Rotha 'thought' about any given situation.

According to Nesta, Rotha was very comfortable in the company of royalty and the upper tiers of society, was well schooled in the art of mixing with the gentry and was fully accustomed to the behaviour expected of her at all levels of society. However it was scouting and the Girl Guides that occupied most of her thoughts during her childhood years. It's here that we may sense her mother's domineering character coming to the fore. Their interest in the 'outdoor life' was already present in the two girls, one in which their exposure to *Scouting for Boys* had only served to spur them on to join the movement.

Here we see the first signs that Blanch may be using Rotha as a conduit through whom she might live some of her own life. The two girls, whatever the truth about their being full members of the Boy Scouts, suddenly had a Scout Master in the form of Rotha's mother. There was no good reason why Blanch Lintorn-Orman should not become a Scout Master, and no reason why a troop should be formed with just two members, but the Forest Mere Troop consisting entirely of the Scout Mistress, her daughter and her daughter's companion was not an entirely normal state of affairs.

The same pattern can be seen when Rotha, volunteering for war service, finds herself working under the command of her mother again, this time with the Women's Reserve Ambulance Corps but it's not clear who was the first to join that group. Either way, the mother is in a position of power over the child, a situation that is repeated throughout Rotha's short life.

Based upon other events it may be a correct assumption that Blanch introduced Rotha to the WRAC, with responsibility for transport, as this has echoes of the situation in Bournemouth immediately preceding the war when Blanch, head of district, oversaw Rotha's formation of her own troop of Girl Guides under her mother's guidance. With Blanch's home being its headquarters it seems that Blanch was central to the WRAC, and that Rotha, again, was playing patrol leader to Blanch as scoutmaster.

It was by joining the Scottish Women's Hospital, and serving with that organisation in Serbia, that Rotha was finally to come out from under the shadow of her mother, for a while. Of course it seems that Blanch's circle of friends were probably instrumental in getting her a position with the SWH, but away from Blanch's day-to-day influence. Once with the SWH she metaphorically 'let her hair down' and perhaps we begin to see something of her real character come to the fore.

Strangely, as was mentioned before, she is not featured in any of the books which cover the SWH in Serbia but there is no doubt that she was there, as her name appears in lists of drivers and those evacuated; similarly in books which cover the fire in Thessaloniki and SWH's involvement there. On her return to Britain, her involvement with the Red Cross is mentioned but not reported upon, and her re-locating to Over Langford Manor is a simple matter of fact. The evidence of Francis Wookey is the only personal memory of Rotha that there is on record from this time.

Considering her developing political views and her promoting them as fascist, it is fairer to categorise them as ultra-conservative rather than fascist, for that is what they were. Fascist was a term borrowed from Italy and was adopted because of her admiration for Mussolini's fight against socialism and communism; i.e., his objectives rather than his methods. We should be aware that at this juncture the term was not fully defined and carried none of the overtones which it later bore – overtones of anti-Semitism from which she was at pains to distance herself.

Although presented as her idea alone, there is the continued spectre of her mother's hand in the formation of the British Fascisti, the name again an indication of naivety, and once more a throwback to the aims of ultra-conservatism. The management of the BF was drawn from the ranks, although not exclusively, of Blanch's circle of friends and surprisingly was dominated by men. Had Rotha been the sole advocate there surely would have been a greater role for women, particularly those who she served with in Serbia, in the management of the new group. It is possible that Blanch, and her money, were the innovators and that Rotha was simply the 'front': the mouthpiece.

The story of Rotha and the BF is one of a continual struggle for survival and continuity, first the name, then the losing of membership for her uncompromising attitude over the Organisation for the Maintenance of Supplies and loss of autonomy and finally the pressure to adopt an anti-Semitic policy. As far as is possible to tell, Rotha did blame the Jewish financiers for aiding and abetting the Bolsheviks, but not the Jews as a race of people.

Blakeney and Leese left the BF and eventually joined Oswald Mosley in his campaign to align with Adolph Hitler. Rotha and the BF became more sidelined and isolated. In the end her mother's funds ran low and she sank further in decline; not only as a political leader, but as a healthy young woman. She died alone, away from her country of birth and far removed from any family.

She will be forever known as the woman who formed the first fascist group in Britain, an untrue legacy. More accurately the woman who formed the first group that included the word 'fascist' in its name. A word that was ill defined at the time and later went on to mean something quite different. A better name, a more appropriate name, a name that better described Rotha Lintorn-Orman's real purpose would have been THE BRITISH LOYALISTS.

# Appendix

Additional information on a variety of subjects mentioned briefly in the text which is better explained away from the main narrative, either because it covers aspects which are relevant to the greater understanding for the reader, or because it spans more than one chapter and so requires a less specific location within the narrative.

## Robert Baden-Powell

Robert Baden-Powell, whose book made such an impression on Rotha and Nesta, was a real life hero of the Boer wars, specifically the Siege of Mafeking. He had joined the 13th Hussars in India in 1876, then served in Africa in Natal Province and then posted to Malta as military secretary and senior aide-de-camp to the Commander-in-Chief and the Governor. He also worked as an intelligence officer for the Director of Military Intelligence in the Mediterranean, often travelling in disguise.

Baden-Powell returned to Africa in 1896 and was involved in the siege in Bulawayo where he commanded reconnaissance missions into enemy territory, and where he formed many of the ideas that he would eventually employ in the formation of the Boy Scouts and also to some extent the Girl Guides. It was while in Africa that he was accused and tried for illegally executing a prisoner of war, but Baden-Powell was cleared and he walked from court 'without a stain on my character'. Many of his co-officers disagreed the findings of the military court.

Baden-Powell was involved in the Siege of Mafeking where he and his troops were besieged for 217 days. The siege was not well maintained by the Boers and Baden-Powell's troops were able to harass them on numerous wide patrols, Baden-Powell undertaking much of that work himself. During the siege, the Mafeking Cadet Corps, made up of boys below fighting age, stood guard and carried messages, freeing grown men to fight. He was sufficiently impressed with them that he used them as a model for his later deliberations.

When the siege was eventually lifted Baden-Powell was lauded as a popular hero. By the time he returned to Britain in 1903 he was already known to the public and was the hero of every adventure loving boy in the country. He was the epitome of the derring-do *Boys Own* adventurer. His publications, first aimed at grown men, and then later at boys, found unexpected popularity. Nesta's autobiography suggests that not only Baden-Powell's book was new to Rotha and Nesta, but so was knowledge of Baden-Powell himself.

> We were taking in a weekly paper called The Scout and several references to enrolments seemed to make it clear that girls could not be Scouts.[1]

A clearer interpretation of the situation might be, more accurately, that Rotha and Nesta, like most young people of that time, were very familiar with Baden-Powell, his reputation and the scouting movement. The revelation that came to them was the contents of Baden-Powell's book, which they read avidly, and the path that it led them along. It would appear that much of the contents of *Scouting for Boys* was already something that they had already mastered, or was within their grasp.

## The Suffragettes

The Suffragette movement began life in 1903 under the auspices of Emmeline Pankhurst as the Women's Social and Political Union (WSPU), a militant group of women campaigning for women's suffrage. The term Suffragette was first coined by the *Daily Mail* as a term of ridicule, but the comment backfired and the WSPU began to use the term to its own advantage.

The 'suffragette' movement began its operations in and around Manchester area disrupting speeches by Churchill and others. They were arrested and charged but preferred to go to gaol rather than pay their fines. Even at this early stage there was a stereotypical view of the suffragette as a strong minded women in masculine clothes, an image that matched the reality of the SWH drivers in the field, especially to be seen in Serbia, but before that in other Western European theatres of war.

As a matter of principle the WSPU issued instructions that members should present themselves in feminine attire whenever they appeared in their role of suffragette. Pankhurst even went as far as designing jewellery and other items in WSPU colours to satisfy that end; fashionable ladies even took to wearing purple, white and green favours with their normal dress to show solidarity.

After 1912 the WSPU tactics became more militant, including smashing windows and escalating to arson and the detonation of explosive and incendiary devices. One famous incident, attempting to interfere with the 1913 Derby at Epsom, resulted in the suffragette's death. There were unsuccessful attempts to have the suffragettes classed as political prisoners, they were instead classed as 'common criminals' and treated as such, with few privileges.

It has been suggested that Emmeline Pankhurst could be compared to Hitler and Mussolini in using the WSPU as the vehicle by which she promoted herself as might a fascist leader. The WSPU was funded by a few wealthy families, it used bombing and arson to further its cause, and it relied on the cult of personality to advance the standing and reputation of its leader – Emmeline Pankhurst.

The abandonment of the fight for women's suffrage at the outbreak of war left many of her followers without a cause to pursue and without a leader to follow. There were others who could provide leadership, but within a limited field such as SWH, but lacking the appeal of a wider campaign. There were many young and militant women who had seen Emmeline Pankhurst as their leader, with a clearly defined cause for which to fight, but who now had been set adrift. When the war was ended they would look to a new cause. If the fight for women's suffrage was won they would need to take up their cudgels for another cause - fascism.

## The British Union of Fascists

The British Union of Fascists developed out of Oswald Mosley's original New Party and had been met with considerable popular support following the 1932 General Election, followed by the Olympia rally two years later. It was at this rally that the first signs of brutality among the BUF supporters was seen by the population at large, and in the light of this the BUF began to see its wider support wane.

During these early years, before Rotha's death, there was considerable animosity between the BUF and BF, to the point of open warfare on the streets. One by one, the extant fascist groups, under Blakeney, Leese and others threw their lot in with Mosley and the BUF, to the point when Rotha Lintorn-Orman was the sole voice on the fascist wing still prepared to resist. This was the signal for an all-out war between the two, a war that Rotha could have no realistic expectation of winning.

By the time of her death in 1935 those who had left the BF, either to join other fascist groups or start movements of their own, had fallen under the spell of Mosley with his pro-German stance. Mosley's position could even be said to be anti-British, later to be shown in his support for Edward VII, Mrs Simpson and the German leader. Mosley's anti-Semitic rhetoric was at odds with Rotha's interpretation of fascism, which seemed not to feature in her own beliefs.

Surprisingly, her last staunch supporter Viscountess Downe, having stayed with Rotha until the BF was finally 'wound up' shortly after her death, eventually joined Mosley, putting herself forward as a BUF candidate at the election which was cancelled because the Second World War was approaching. Unlike Mosley, and hundreds of his supporters, the Viscountess was never interred, but received plenty of police attention.

# Notes

## Chapter 1

1. GRO 1895 Q1 Kensington 1a/147
2. GRO 1893 Q3 Kensington 1a/252
3. Rosie Llewellyn-Jones, *Chowkidar*, British Association For Cemeteries In South Asia, Volume 12 Number 1 Spring 2009
4. TNA Census Class: RG12; Piece: 24; Folio: 11; Page: 15
5. Somerset Heritage Service; Ref: D\P\chl/2/1/7
6. TNA Census Class: RG12; Piece: 1956; Folio: 144; Page: 13
7. Captain R.S.S. Baden-Powell, *Reconnaissance and Scouting*, William Clowes and Sons, 1891
8. Lydia Becker, *Contemporary Review*, 1867

## Chapter 2

1. COW Archive ASEG/PR/4/1 #7
2. GRO 1893 Q3 Kensington 1a/252
3. *Daily Malta Chronicle* and *Garrison Gazette* – Wednesday, 23 February 1898
4. *Daily Telegraph & Courier* (London) – Friday, 24 November 1899
5. Erskine Childers, *The Riddle of the Sands*, Smith, Elder & Co, 1903
6. Kaiser Wilhelm II, *Speech to the North German Regatta Association*, 1901
7. TNA Census Class: RG13; Piece: 1040; Folio: 113; Page: 85
8. TNA Census Class: RG13; Piece: 2341; Folio: 107; Page: 7

9. GRO 1901 Q4 Long Ashton 5c/412
10. National Probate Calendar (Index of Wills and Administrations), 1858-1995
11. Colonel Sir Charles M. Watson, *The History of the Corps of Royal Engineers*, Chatham, 1954
12. A discharge of a cannon repeated at intervals of a minute usually in connection with the funeral of a general or flag officer
13. *Western Daily Press* – Thursday, 19 February 1903
14. National Probate Calendar (Index of Wills and Administrations), 1858-1995

## Chapter 3

1. Nesta Maude Ashworth, Mary Ashworth and Margaret Spencer, *A Guiding Life*, Friesen Press, 2015
2. Nesta Maude Ashworth, Mary Ashworth and Margaret Spencer, *A Guiding Life*, Friesen Press, 2015
3. A blend of merino wool and cotton, first trademarked fabric in the world, offering warmth and durability.
4. A gig is a clinker built rowing boat, but also fitted with a small mast for sailing down wind
5. Nesta Maude Ashworth
6. Uncle of Wilbert Awdry, later to become the creator of *Thomas the Tank Engine*
7. Robert Baden-Powell, *Scouting for Boys*, 1908

## Chapter 4

1. Nesta Maude Ashworth, Mary Ashworth and Margaret Spencer, *A Guiding Life*, Friesen Press, 2015
2. Nesta Maude Ashworth, Mary Ashworth and Margaret Spencer, *A Guiding Life*, Friesen Press, 2015
3. Helen D. Gardner, *The First Girl Guide*, Amberly Publishing, 2010
4. *Ibid*

## Chapter 5

1. Anthony J. Randall, *Edith Cavell, Brussels via Yorc*, Cloister House Press, 2015
2. *Staffordshire Advertiser* – Saturday, 19 December 1914
3. Young women who behave in a boisterously assertive or crude manner, Concise Oxford Dictionary
4. *London Evening Standard* – Friday, 10 September 1915
5. *Daily News* (London) – Thursday, 16 September 1915
6. M.A. Edgington, *Bournemouth and the First World War*, Bournemouth Local Studies Publications, 1985

## Chapter 6

1. Leah Leneman, *In the Service of Life*, Mercat Press, 1994
2. Leah Leneman, *In the Service of Life*, Mercat Press, 1994
3. Lady Frances Balfour, *Dr Elsie Inglis*, Hodder and Stoughton, 1919
4. Anthony J. Randall, *Edith Cavell, Brussels via Yorc*, Cloister House Press, 2015
5. Lucy Inglis, *Elsie Inglis, the Suffragette Physician*, The Lancet, 2014
6. Vera Holme, *Account of the work of Evelina Haverfield in Serbia*, London University, c.1920
7. *Dundee Courier* – Thursday. 10 August 1916

## Chapter 7

1. inverted = lesbian
2. Rachel Michelle Brown, *Women and World War One: Perspectives on Women's Role in s Role in WWI Literature*, Central Washington University, 2021
3. Leah Leneman, *In the Service of Life*, Mercat Press, 1994
4. Leah Leneman, *In the Service of Life*, Mercat Press, 1994

## Chapter 8

1. E. Morrison and C. Parry, *The Scottish Women's Hospitals for Foreign Service*, Royal College of Physicians of Edinburgh, 2014
2. Georgina Cooper, Thomson Reuters, 2009
3. David Shillito, *The Great Fire of 1917: an eyewitness account*, Salonika Campaign Society, 2017
4. David Shillito, *The Great Fire of 1917: an eyewitness account*, Salonika Campaign Society, 2017
5. Francis Wookey, *Personal thoughts about Miss R Lintorn Orman of Over Langford Manor*, Somerset Heritage Centre, DD/X/AUS/179, 2003
6. *Socialist* (Edinburgh) – Thursday, 10 November 1921
7. *Kentish Independent* – Friday, 14 July 1922

## Chapter 9

1. Adolph Hitler, Munich 1922
2. John Wittam, *Fascist Italy*, Manchester University Press, 1995
3. *The Luton News*, 24 July 1919
4. John Wittam, Fascist Italy, Manchester University Press, 1995
5. *The Times* (London, England), 12 August 1922

## Chapter 10

1. *The Times* (London, England), 3 November 1922
2. *Daily News* (London) – Tuesday, 2 January 1923
3. Alan Percy, *The Patriot*, 9 February 1922
4. Nesta Webster, *The Patriot*, 9 February 1922
5. Anon, The Patriot, 16 February 1922
6. Sir Percival Phillips, *The Red Dragon and the Black Shirts*, Carmelite House, 1922
7. *The Patriot*, 22 June 1922

## Chapter 11

1. Robert Speaight, *The Life Of Hilaire Belloc*, Hollis & Carter, 1957
2. *Daily Herald* – Friday, 31 August 1923

## Chapter 12

1. Steven Woodbridge, *Early Interwar Assessments of the Nature of British Fascism in the 1920s*, Bologna on line, 2019, https://storiaefuturo.eu/reaction-or-revolution-early-interwar-assessments-of-the-nature-of-british-fascism-in-the-1920s/
2. Martin Durham, *Women, Gender and Fascism in Europe, edited by Kevin Passmore*, Manchester University Press, 2003
3. *Ibid*
4. *Gloucester Citizen*, *Hull Daily Mail* – Monday, 22 March 1926
5. *Yorkshire Post* and *Leeds Intelligencer* – Monday, 11 October 1926 (#25)
6. *Hull Daily Mail* - Thursday, 5 May 1927 #26
7. Jason Stanley, *How Fascism Works*, Random House, 2018

## Chapter 13

1. Thomas Linehan, *British fascism 1918-39, Parties, ideology and Culture*, Manchester University Press, 2000
2. The Workers Bulletin, *Fascist Impudence*, The Communist Party of Great Britain, 1926
3. Keith Layboun, *The General Strike, Day by Day*, Sutton Publishing Ltd, 1996
4. Hair cut in the style of a bob
5. *Daily News* (London) – Thursday, 11 November 1926

## Chapter 14

1. Francis Wookey, *Personal thoughts about Miss R Lintorn Orman of Over Langford Manor*, Somerset Heritage Centre, DD/X/AUS/179, 2003

2. Francis Wookey, *Personal thoughts about Miss R Lintorn Orman of Over Langford Manor*, Somerset Heritage Centre, DD/X/AUS/179, 2003
3. Martin Pugh, *Hurrah for the Blackshirts*, Random House
4. Martin Pugh, *Hurrah for the Blackshirts*, Random House
5. *St. Pancras Gazette* – Friday, 12 October 1928

## Chapter 15

1. Ulster refers to the nine counties of the historic province, three of which remained part of Great Britain
2. *East London Observer* – Saturday, 2 July 1927
3. *Ballymena Weekly Telegraph* – Saturday, 13 April 1935 #30
4. Anne de Courcy, *Diana Mosley*, Chatto & Windus, 2003

## Chapter 16

1. Nesta Maude Ashworth, Mary Ashworth and Margaret Spencer, *A Guiding Life*, Friesen Press, 2015

# Index